"*Bee's Brilliant Biscuits* oozes creativity and is the only biscuit book you will ever need. It has opened up biscuity avenues I never knew existed and I'm going to eat my way around them one by one!"

Luis Troyano, Great British Bake Off finalist 2014

BEE'S
BRILLIANT
BISCUITS

BEE'S BRILLIANT BISCUITS

BEE BERRIE

PAVILION

To my mum Sandra, who hates cooking and baking, but can do the job of both mum and dad very well – ah love you hen!

CONTENTS

INTRODUCTION

Welcome biscuit-bothering friends, fellow cookie creators and baking 'badasses', you have found it! You have discovered the holy grail of biscuit baking, the one and only recipe book to guarantee you baked cookie kryptonite!

Let's face it, cookies and biscuits are everything that cupcakes are not. Anyone worth his or her baking salt can knock out a cute little cupcake, or a signature sponge these days. To stand out from the home-baking crowd, you will have to throw a ton of expensive ingredients at the problem and risk carpal tunnel syndrome to perfect your icing swirl!

Not so with biscuits and cookies – these babies are full on fun. Quicker, easier and way more versatile than their cakey counterparts, biscuits have short and sweet bake times, they last for ages, and any leftover dough or cookies can be frozen for delayed gratification – in other words, total winners.

No matter what you crave, this cookie compendium teaches you everything – from a super-easy vanilla 'parent' dough, to classics like gooey chocolate cookies or soft honey and oatmeal cookies. I have even given away the secret to my award-winning jammy dodger recipe and there are also some recipes that require an artistic eye and a crafty edge too.

This book covers all the core information needed to make you into a biscuit baking boss! There are recipes for beautiful birthday cookie cakes, amazing gingerbread houses, perfect wedding favour ideas and even a recipe for your four-legged doggy friend. If you are looking for adventure, I have a really fun recipe for BBQ Bacon Biscotti (p.116), along with my Trash Can Cookie (p.41) as well!

My biscuit baking commandments (pp.8–9) provide useful tips to give novice bakers a head start. And for those who are a bit more experienced, there are some useful prompts to help you find design, colour and flavour inspiration, so you can adapt my recipes and make them your own.

Being in the kitchen is a bit of escapism for me and it's always been my 'happy place'. I find cooking and baking so fun, relaxing and totally rewarding, so I hope I can share some of my 'bake love' with you, and I hope this book inspires you to roll up your sleeves, exercise your baking muscles, get your creative cap on and start baking biscuits!

You can get in touch and ask questions on Twitter @bees bakery, and I'd love to see pictures of your creations on Instagram @beesbakery, so tag me using #BeesBiscuits

BEE'S BISCUITTY COMMANDMENTS!

1. Stay chilled – always roll your cookie dough from cold, and rechill before baking for super-sharp clean-edged biscuits and cookies.

2. Get some baking biceps! Engage your abs and arm muscles, don't cheat with a mixer. After all, you are going to have a couple of extra calories to burn off!

3. Don't be scared to get your (clean) hands into the bowl! Often its quicker than mixing with a spoon, and you will get a feel for what makes a good consistency of dough too.

4. Turn your dough as you roll, or roll in different directions, to ensure that you are accounting for any differences in pressure points and you get a nice even dough height.

5. Bake different sized cookies on different trays – smaller cookies need less time than big ones, so use your noggin and keep them on different trays so you don't end up with little burnt ones and big soft ones.

6. Don't overwork yourself, or your dough. Too much kneading and rerolling of your dough will result in cracked and misshapen cookies. To avoid this, always cut as many cookies from the first and second roll out of dough as possible, and consider freezing your third roll out before baking.

7. Improvise with your kit – so what if you don't have the snazziest new cookie cutter, make your own! Use the rim of a mug, or a clean jam jar to cut out rounds, or a kitchen knife to cut out squares. Who cares if you don't have a collection of posh fabric piping bags? Make your own out of Ziploc bags.

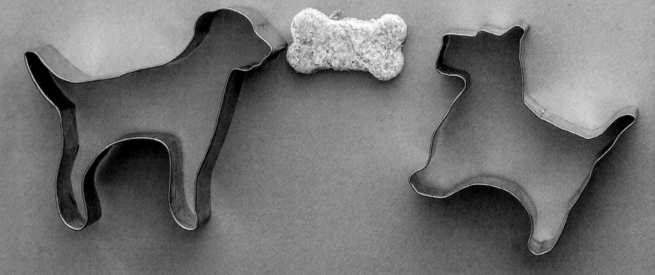

8. Get the tunes on! A baking playlist will keep you going when the bake gets tough.

9. Always taste and test as you go along. When baking a recipe for the first time, try to bake one cookie before you do the whole batch, to sense-check and correct any mistakes.

10. Don't be afraid to tidy up your bakes when they come out the oven – cut off any burnt bits, straighten up a wonky edge with a cheese grater or hide any knobbly bits with an icing and make all your bakes look beautiful!

11. Care for the environment – avoid using foil at all costs, it takes 100 years to biodegrade and there are alternatives. Use fair-trade EVERYTHING, recycled kitchen paper and biodegradable clingfilm.

12. Get thrifty – freeze extra dough or broken biscuits and use them later (see p.44 for ideas of what to do with them).

13. If you can, clear a shelf in the fridge/freezer for chilling your dough.

14. Get friendly with your oven – understand its hot spots and avoid baking cookies on the corresponding part of your baking tray.

15. Invest in some highbrow pieces of kit if you can – get yourself a nice new baking tray and good-quality parchment paper – it will make all the difference. Get some attractive plastic containers or tins to keep your bakes fresh and tasty for as long as possible.

16. Get busy! Be creative; make your own cookie cutter templates on cardboard (then cut around them with the tip of a sharp knife), try new flavour combinations and play with colours.

17. Make your bakes into gifts – this will make you very popular and stop you getting a baker's bum!

18. Keep frozen balls of dough in an egg box in the freezer so you can bake a treat at short notice.

19. If you don't have a rolling pin, you can use a strong, clean glass bottle instead.

20. Always use free-range eggs. Healthier hens lay better eggs.

INTRODUCING FLAVOURS & CREATIVITY

Chefs, sommeliers and experimental home cooks are used to thinking about pairing flavours and tastes to try to create new, mind-blowing combinations. There's no reason why you can't too.

The general aim in combining flavours is one of these:
- To choose two flavours that complement and enhance each other, such as chocolate and coffee.
- To choose two (or more) flavours that contrast with each other, to create a taste explosion, or just to mellow each other out a little e.g. lemon and lavender.

When baking cookies and biscuits, we are normally slightly limited by using dry or dried ingredients, but that doesn't mean we can't incorporate new tastes by incorporating herbs into sugar, or infusing flavours into butter, and even mixing powders or seasonings into icing.

There are a few interesting flavour combos in this book, such as the Bacon and Chocolate Chip Cookies (p.113), the Sea Salt and Burnt Butter Cookies (p.29) and the Tangerine and Thyme Cookies (p.24). I want to encourage you to experiment with flavours, and maybe even try a few new ones to see what really rocks your baking world!

The chart opposite is a 'starter for 10' which I hope will show you a few combinations that you have not tried before, and inspire you to add more. I have included basic instructions on how to build these combinations into baking, so roll up your sleeves, get your baking muscle on show, and create something awesome!

Source of flavour	Example	Goes well with	Add it to your baking by...
Herbs and flowers	Rosemary, thyme, basil	Citrus notes e.g. lemon, orange, tangerine	Chopping finely and mixing in with the butter and sugar, or infuse with the sugar overnight for a stronger flavour. Sprinkle individual leaves on top of icing.
	Lavender, rose essence or petals, orange flower water	Dairy frostings, nutty flavours, vanilla	Cream a couple of drops it with the butter and sugar or sprinkle dried petals on top of icing.
Seasoning and spices	Sea salt	Brown sugar, chocolate, bittersweet flavours	Use salted butter for extra flavour in recipes, sprinkle a few sea salt flakes on top after baking, create a salted caramel by cooking your butter before use.
	Ground peppercorns	Chocolate, dark brown sugar, spices, dairy frosting	Crack fresh peppercorns into your gingerbread hot mix, using pink peppercorns on top of your dairy frosting.
	Cardamom, cinnamon, ground ginger, nutmeg and cloves	Sugars, dairy frosting, chocolate	Add to flour before mixing dough, cook them in a hot mix with the sugar, add a little to your buttercream.
	Chilli	Cheesy biscuits (cookies), brown sugar, spices, coffee and chocolate	Add sparingly to a chocolate buttercream or add a few flakes to the dough of a cheesy biscuit (cookie).
Citrus fruits	Lemon zest, orange zest, bergamot zest	Herbs (see above), fresh red fruits e.g. raspberries, dairy	Add zest to buttercream or sprinkle on top of drizzled icing, add into a chocolate frosting. (See above for more ideas).
Red fruits	Raspberries, strawberries	Chocolate, dairy frosting, other fruits e.g. citrus	Add richness to a chocolate dough. Use dried fruit in oat recipes
Nuts and nut butters	Peanut, hazelnut, cashew nut butter	Chocolate	Add richness to a chocolate dough, add to a buttercream for a crunchy frosting.
Vanilla	Vanilla bean extract or real pods (beans)	Almost everything! Dairy frostings, floral notes, nuts, fruits and most types of dough	Add to most cookie dough recipes to add depth of flavour. Add into most frostings to create a speckled finish.

GIVING COOKIES AS GIFTS

If you are in a truly committed relationship with baking (!), you will never have to spend your hard-earned money on a gift again! I very rarely buy presents, but instead try to create something unique and personal (and of course baked) for each person. Here are a few questions and prompts to help your creativity flow and make you the best present giver in town!

Questions to prompt ideas

- Who is the gift for? Do you want to impress them, or just treat them?
- What's their favourite colour/flavour?
- Do they have a favourite band/celebrity crush and could you use this somehow?
- Are they adventurous and would want to try something new?
- Where are they from? Are there any famous bakes or specialities from nearby?
- Where will you give the gift? Will you have to post it or will there be a big party? Will it be more afternoon tea, or midnight nightclub snack?
- How long does it need to keep?
- Is there a new technique you want to try that you can get away with testing out on them?
- Do you have oodles of time, or need something quick and speedy?
- What's their style? Do they go for block colour or patterns and can you work this into the design?
- Is there anyone else you can collaborate with to share the load/create something amazing?
- What's the occasion – is there a theme you can pull from e.g. 30th birthday, new home or engagement?

Could you ...

- Match their favourite colour in cookie icing?
- Cut their name/initials out of a Jammy biscuit?
- Create a cookie pop in the shape of their face?
- Write their favourite word on a speech bubble shaped cookie?
- Give them something to take home at Christmas?
- Commemorate the date with a stamped cookie?
- Add sprinkles/flower petals/edible paper flowers to jazz it up?
- Take inspiration from pinterest or instagram?
- Print their favourite picture or design onto edible paper?
- Choose beautiful packaging to really impress?
- Make them a birthday cake out of giant cookies, filled with icing of their favourite colour?
- Give them a painted egg box of frozen cookies with the baking instructions on a notecard?
- Bake a special veggie or vegan recipe just for them.

TIPS FOR BAKING WITH KIDS

• Expect a mess! Think about putting newspaper over the work surface to make clearing up very easy. If your child is really little, consider putting them into their highchair and using the attached tray as their work surface – they can roll dough, add sprinkles and do all sorts of jobs here and spill will be limited.

• Choose one-bowl wonder recipes – they are easier to manage and if you pre-measure all your ingredients in advance, they can just be tipped into the big bowl by the little person.

• Invest in an apron for yourself and your little one, then roll up sleeves and tie their hair back.

• Consider investing in a kid's baking kit – with mini versions of wooden spoons, plastic bowls and a little rolling pin.

• Divide up the jobs – remember that under fives can help with certain jobs like chopping bananas with a kid's knife, or mashing them up with a potato masher, using a cookie cutter on pre-rolled dough, cracking eggs or adding sprinkles.

• Make your dough in advance so it's ready to roll and cut before you start.

• Invest in some fun, but easy to use cutters. Animal shapes are great as long as they are not too complicated a shape – you don't want pieces that will easily get deformed or burn when baking.

• Let them do it themselves – one bit of dough for you and one bit for them. This way they will get to have fun, and you will end up with some prettier cookies to save too.

• When decorating, create a sprinkle zone inside a large baking tray or plastic container – this will minimise sprinkle spillage.

BEE'S RECIPES

VANILLA SUGAR COOKIES

MAKES 10

140g/5oz/scant ⅔ cup cold salted butter,
  cut into pieces
280g/10oz/2 cups plain (all-purpose) flour,
  sifted, plus extra for dusting
140g/5oz/scant ¾ cup caster (superfine) or
  soft brown sugar
1 egg
1 tsp vanilla extract

To jazz up your dough, try these additions:

- grated zest of 1 lemon/lime/tangerine/
  orange
- if you're feeling really adventurous, combine
  a herb with the citrus as follows:
  lemon and 1 tbsp chopped fresh basil or
  mint leaves;
  orange and 1 heaped tsp fresh rosemary
  or thyme
- substitute the vanilla for almond essence or
  coconut oil
- 1 tbsp chopped dried rose petals or
  2 tsp chopped culinary grade lavender
- melt the butter with 2 tsp teabag contents,
  mix well and allow to set before using – Earl
  Grey or English Breakfast taste great, but
  chai tea also works brilliantly
- for a super-quick gingerbread hack, add
  1 tsp ground ginger and 1 tsp ground
  cinnamon, plus 1 tbsp treacle and a pinch of
  allspice or nutmeg at the beginning
- add a generous handful of chocolate chips at
  the final stage before rolling and cutting out
  your dough

Every baker needs a great, basic cookie recipe in their baking repertoire, and this is it!

Using your fingertips, crush the butter and flour together in a large bowl until it resembles fine breadcrumbs. Add the sugar (and any of your optional additions) and mix with a wooden spoon until it is just combined. Add the egg and vanilla and mix until a fairly firm dough forms – it will be slightly sticky to the touch.

Squeeze the dough into a flat sausage shape, and sandwich it between 2 sheets of clingfilm. Using a rolling pin, roll it out until it is about 2cm/¾in thick, then chill in the refrigerator for at least 30 minutes to harden up.

Roll out the dough on a lightly floured surface until it is 1.5cm/⅜in thick, then using a cookie cutter of your choice, cut out as many shapes as you can. Transfer the cut cookies to a baking sheet lined with parchment paper and chill in the refrigerator for 20 minutes.

Preheat the oven to 170°C/338°F/Gas mark 3. Pop the cold baking tray directly into the oven and bake the cookies for 7–10 minutes, or until starting to turn golden at the edges, while the middles still have a bit of squidge. Cool the cookies on a wire rack before decorating.

To create a cookie pop, insert a lollipop stick into the middle of your cookie before baking, and use stamps and sprinkles to decorate. Try baking different shapes for different themes, e.g. Christmas stars, or Valentine hearts.

Emboss your cookies with a brilliant, kid-friendly rolling pin – I use one with a super-cool dinosaur design on it.

YOUR GO-TO SHORTBREAD RECIPE

MAKES 16–20
200g/7oz/scant 1 cup cold
   butter, cut into cubes
260g/9oz/scant 2 cups plain
   (all-purpose) flour, plus
   extra for dusting

20g/¾oz/scant ¼ cup rice flour
20g/¾oz/scant ¼ cup cornflour (cornstarch)
100g/3½oz/scant 1 cup icing (confectioners') sugar
1 egg yolk
½ tsp vanilla bean extract
2 tbsp caster (superfine) sugar, for dusting (optional)

I'm a Scottish lassie by birth, so my Glaswegian mum would kill me if I didn't have a great shortbread recipe in my book. This one's for you hen!

Put the butter and all the flours into a large bowl and, using your fingertips, crush the butter and flours together until it looks like sandy breadcrumbs. Add the icing sugar, sifting it if there are any lumps, and mix with a wooden spoon until it is just combined. Add the egg yolk and vanilla and mix with the spoon until a smooth, fairly firm dough forms. If it is too crumbly, warm your hands and knead it gently in the bowl to heat up the butter and bring it all together, but avoid kneading it for too long.

Squeeze the dough into a flat sausage shape, and sandwich it between 2 sheets of clingfilm. Using a rolling pin, roll it out until it is about 2cm/¾in thick, then chill in the refrigerator for 30 minutes.

Line a baking sheet with parchment paper.

Roll out the dough on a lightly floured surface to your desired thickness. Shortbread dough can be sticky, so remember to lift the sheet up and flour underneath it as well as on top.

There are lots of different ways to shape a good shortbread, from long thin fingers to large rounds, and this recipe will work with all of these. My preferred style is small fat circles, which I like to then finish with a few embossed dots around the edge, made with a cocktail stick or the end of a chopstick.

Using your cutter of choice, cut out as many rounds as you can, then transfer the cut cookies onto the lined baking sheet with a palette knife and chill again for 20 minutes.

Preheat the oven to 170°C/338°F/Gas mark 3.

Dust the tops with caster sugar and bake in the oven for 7–10 minutes for smaller biscuits, and about 10–12 minutes for larger ones. If you choose to bake 1 large round, you will need to increase the baking time to about 15–20 minutes but you will know they are done as they will start to just turn golden brown at the edges. Allow to cool on a wire rack.

LEMON SUGAR ROLL COOKIES

MAKES AT LEAST 10 COOKIES
1 batch Vanilla Sugar Cookie dough (p.18) with
  zest of 1 lemon added
sprinkles, nuts or seeds of your choice

Keeping a roll of cookie dough in your freezer means you can have a hot cookie snack available at any time you like, at about 10 minutes notice – the ultimate home comfort food! As soon as your child is at a suitable age, pre-cut the cookie logs into pieces and they can then bake themselves a quick snack with minimal mess and fuss.

Divide the dough into 2 or 3 balls then roll each one into a fat regular sausage shape in the palms of your hands. Be gentle with the dough. Cover and chill the dough in the refrigerator for about 20 minutes to set the shape, then roll again to make a nice, crisp circular shape.

Put a square of parchment paper or clingfilm onto the work surface and sprinkle your chosen nuts, seeds or sprinkles in an even layer. Gently roll the dough cylinder in the seeds to embed them into the dough. Add more as needed to ensure a good even coverage. Wrap in clingfilm, chill for 1 hour, then cut into 2cm/¾in discs. Rewrap and freeze for up to 1 month.

Whenever you fancy a cookie, preheat the oven to 175°F/347°F/Gas mark 4 and line a baking tray with parchment paper. Remove as many discs as you'd like from the freezer, place on the lined baking tray and bake from frozen for about 10 minutes, or until the edges turn slightly golden brown. Allow to cool on a wire rack or work surface.

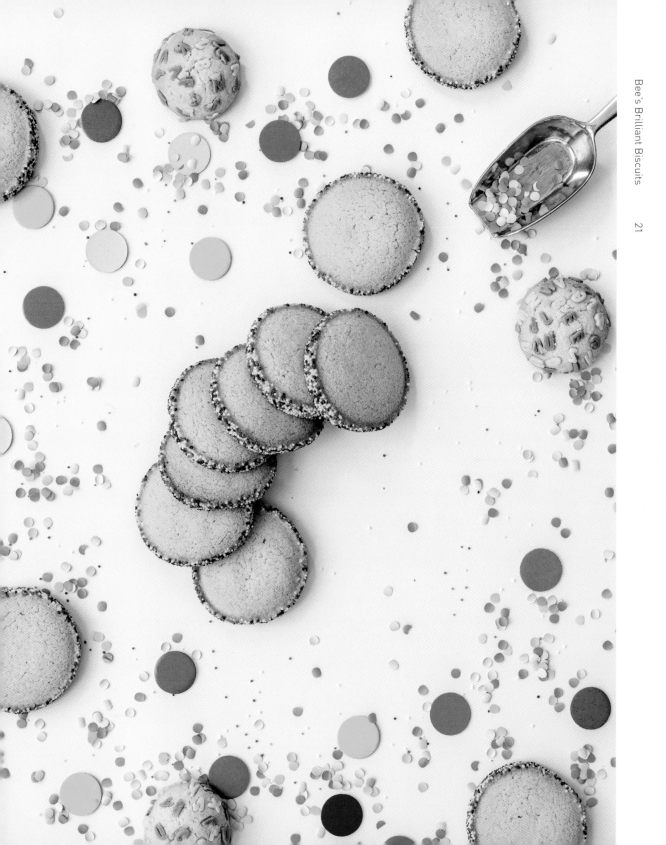

GLUTEN-FREE CITRUS SHORTBREAD

MAKES ABOUT 10–12 BISCUITS
175g/6oz/¾ cup cold salted butter, cut into pieces
100g/3½oz/generous 1 cup ground almonds
5g/¼oz xanthan gum
50g/1¾oz/½ cup gram flour (ground chickpeas)
50g/1¾oz/scant ½ cup pre-mixed plain gluten-free
   flour or rice flour, plus extra for dusting
100g/3½oz/½ cup caster (superfine) sugar
grated zest of 2 lemons, or 1 orange and 1 lemon
1 tsp vanilla bean paste
3 drops of lemon or orange essence
1 egg

The problem with baking with pre-mixed gluten-free flour is that it often leaves biscuits tasting like a mouthful of sand! I'm yet to find a brand of gluten-free flour that tastes delicious, no matter what you bake – it's the holy grail of gluten-free baking! What I have found though, is that combining several different types of gluten-free flour is the way to a non-gritty biscuit, so that's what I have done here, with this fab lemon shortbread.

Put the butter, ground almonds, xanthan gum and flours in a large bowl and, using your fingertips, crush the butter and mix into the rest of the ingredients in the bowl until it resembles a breadcrumb-like mixture. Add the caster sugar, citrus zest, vanilla, citrus essence and egg and mix until a dough is formed. If the butter is very cold, you may find it easier to get your hands into the bowl as this will heat the mixture up slightly and bring it together more easily.

Squeeze the dough into a flat sausage shape, and sandwich it between 2 sheets of clingfilm. Using a rolling pin, roll it out until it is about 2cm/¾in thick, then chill in the refrigerator for about 20 minutes to harden up.

Preheat the oven to 175°C/347°F/Gas mark 4 and line a baking tray with parchment paper.

Roll out the dough on a work surface lightly floured with gluten-free flour then cut out regular shapes, such as rounds or squares, or thicker fingers – whatever takes your fancy!

Transfer your shapes to the lined baking tray, and chill again for 5 minutes before baking in the oven for 8–12 minutes. Smaller or thinner shapes will take less time than the bigger or fatter shapes. You will know when they are done when the edges are starting to take a little bit of colour. Allow to cool on the tray before eating.

TANGERINE AND THYME DRIZZLES

MAKES AT LEAST 30 COOKIES

For the cookies
460g/1lb/3¼ cups plain (all-purpose) flour
60g/2¼oz/⅔ cup ground almonds
1½ tsp baking powder
150ml/5fl oz/⅔ cup olive oil
170g/6oz/¾ cup very soft butter (just on the verge of melting, a sunny window ledge is good for this)
300g/10½oz/1½ cups caster (superfine) sugar, plus 2 tsp for rolling

2 eggs
grated zest of 2–3 tangerines, or to taste
1 tsp orange essence (optional)
1 heaped tbsp finely chopped fresh thyme leaves

For the glaze (optional)
140g/5oz/1¼ cups icing (confectioners') sugar
2–3 tbsp tangerine juice
1 tbsp finely chopped fresh thyme leaves, plus extra for decorating (optional)
grated zest of tangerine, to decorate (optional)

This is a cute one-bowl wonder of a recipe that is perfect for freezing in balls for baking later. It can be easily adapted, so if you are feeling adventurous then split your basic dough into two or three portions and flavour each one separately. Other combinations that work are lemon and basil, tangerine and lavender, lemon and fennel, choc chip and mint – have a play!

For the cookies, put all the ingredients into a very large bowl and stir slowly but firmly with a wooden spoon until combined. When fully mixed, separate about half of the mixture into one bowl, spread it to the edges of the bowl, cover with clingfilm and chill in the refrigerator for about 20 minutes.

Meanwhile, with clean hands, form lots of small round balls with the other half of the mixture – they should be just bigger than a golf ball. These can be rolled in a little caster sugar and frozen. I usually chill them on a baking tray before freezing, so they keep their spherical shape when frozen. They keep for

up to a month. A lovely way of storing these is to cut rounds of parchment paper about 10cm/4in across, and rest each little ball inside the troughs of an empty egg box lined with the parchment circles, then freeze – this also makes a pretty gift.

To bake from frozen, preheat the oven to 175°C/328°F/Gas mark 4 and line a baking tray with parchment paper.

Pop the balls onto the lined baking tray. If baking from frozen bake for about 12–15 minutes, or 10–12 minutes if baking from chilled, until the edges just start to turn golden brown. Cool on a wire rack.

If you want to drizzle the balls with glaze, then put all the glaze ingredients into a small bowl and mix thoroughly with a wooden spoon. When the cookies come out of the oven, cool, then make a small indent with your thumb in the top, and spoon or spread a little of the glaze on top. You can decorate them with a final thyme leaf or some grated tangerine zest, if you like.

LOCAL HONEY, OAT AND RAISIN COOKIES

I was lucky enough to be invited to a wedding in Nova Scotia last summer, and took a road trip from Cape Cod through New England to Canada. This was one of the best trips of my life, not least due to the piles of giant honey oatmeal and raisin cookies on the counters of gas stations all over the region – I love them!

Creating a recipe that works was tough, as they are not an easy cookie to master, and everyone has their own preference for how gooey and soft they like them, but this is a good starter. Feel free to add in more or less fruit, and increase or decrease the bake time to get the perfect cookie for you.

Melt the honey, milk, vanilla and butter together in a pan, making sure it doesn't boil. When it's warm, tip in the dried fruit, stir and then leave to rest for a few minutes to cool and for the fruit to soak up the liquid.

Add the oats, flour and sugar to the mixture and combine well.

Form the dough into balls – an ice-cream scoop can make this easier, or just use 2 dessertspoons to make regularly sized heaps of mixture – try to make them high in the middle and leave a 4–5cm/1½–2in gap between the biscuits. Chill in the refrigerator for 10 minutes.

Preheat the oven to 175°C/347°F/Gas mark 4.

Pop your cold baking tray directly into the hot oven and bake for 10–12 minutes until the edges are golden brown. The middles will still feel soft at this point. Remove the cookies from the oven and allow to cool on the tray before eating.

MAKES 6–8 GIANT COOKIES
   OR 10 SMALLER ONES
3 tbsp honey (preferably local if you can get it, I use Bermondsey Bee's Honey)
2 tsp milk
1 tsp vanilla bean extract
85g/3oz/6 tbsp butter
50g/13/4oz dried fruit (raisins are great, but cranberries or blueberries are lovely too)
80g/3oz/1 cup rolled oats
80g/3oz/½ cup self-raising wholemeal (whole-wheat) flour
70g/2½oz/generous ⅓ cup soft brown sugar

SEA SALT AND BROWN BUTTER STAMPED COOKIES

MAKES ABOUT 10–12 COOKIES

For the cookies
170g/6oz/¾ cup salted butter
280g/10oz/2 cups plain (all-purpose) flour, plus extra for dusting
165g/5¾oz/generous ¾ cup soft brown sugar
1 egg
1 tsp vanilla extract
1 tsp flaky sea salt

For the icing
250g/9oz or sugarpaste icing
cornflour (cornstarch), for dusting
gel paste colours of your choice

I was asked to make some nautical themed cookies by the BBC for a programme launch and so I used this super-cool ship rubber stamp. I thought the effect of the stamp was so pretty that I tried a few others too – you can use any new rubber stamp you like (I get mine from the English Stamp Company). Pick one that doesn't have too many fine lines in case of smudges, and wash it thoroughly before using.

Line a baking sheet with parchment paper.

Start by making the burnt butter – you will need to let it cool before making the cookie dough, so allow some time for this. Melt the butter in a pan over a medium heat then reduce the heat to low and cook until it is bubbling. Make sure it is not boiling – it will fizz up a little, but that's normal. Swirl the pan every now and again to ensure that the hot butter doesn't catch on the base of the pan too much, but avoid stirring. After a few minutes you will notice that the butter takes on a beautiful rich caramel smell and that the base of the pan will have a few speckles of brown on it – these are the slightly burnt milk solids. You're looking to cook it for about 5 minutes, or until you have a caramel brown mixture with a good number of brown speckles, but no burning smell. Remove from the heat and allow to cool and solidify before chopping or scraping it into more manageable sized pieces.

Put pieces of burnt butter and the flour into a large bowl and, using your fingertips, crush the butter and flour together until it resembles fine breadcrumbs. Add the sugar and mix with a wooden spoon until it is just combined. Add the egg, vanilla and salt flakes and mix until a fairly firm dough forms – it will be slightly sticky to the touch.

Squeeze the dough into a flat sausage shape, and sandwich it between 2 sheets of clingfilm. Using a rolling pin, roll it out until it is about 2cm/¾in thick, then chill in the refrigerator for at least 30 minutes to harden up.

Roll out the dough on a floured surface until it is 1.5cm/⅝in thick, then, using a cookie cutter of your choice, cut out as many shapes as you can. If you don't have any cutters then be creative! Use the rim of a mug, or a clean jam jar to cut out rounds, a kitchen knife to cut out squares, or create your own cardboard template and cut around it with a sharp knife. Transfer the cut cookies to the lined baking sheet with a palette knife and chill again in the refrigerator for 20 minutes.

Preheat the oven 170°C/338°F/Gas mark 3.

Pop your cold baking tray directly into the hot oven and bake for 7–10 minutes, or until there is just a tiny bit of colour at the edges. Allow the cookies to cool on a wire rack before decorating.

To decorate the cookies, you will need a brand-new, unused rubber stamp for these cookies – any design of your choosing. Roll out the sugarpaste icing on a surface or mat dusted with cornflour until it is about 3–5mm/⅛–¼in thick. Using the same cutter as you used for your cookies, cut out as many shapes as you need, with a couple of spares for testing and set aside.

Using some gel paste colour and 1–2 drops of water, paint a square of kitchen paper a couple of layers thick with the colour until it is saturated, but not sopping wet. If using a dark colour, pop your edible paint pad onto the lid of a plastic container, or a flat plate to avoid the colour marking your work surface. Make sure your 'ink' is the right consistency by testing the stamp out on a piece of paper until you have the right level of coverage – you will need the ink pad to be wet and sticky rather than completely wet.

Once you have the right consistency of 'ink', stamp the icing shapes while they are still on the surface. If you end up with any bald patches, or uneven coverage, use a paintbrush with a little colour on the end to paint in any gaps.

Dab a little water onto the top of each of your cookie with a pastry brush, and put the icing tops onto the cookies. Allow to rest for a few hours to set, or if you're in a hurry, pop them into an oven preheated to 50°C/122°F/lowest possible Gas mark for about 10 minutes. Make sure the stamped patterns are dry before packaging.

BEE'S JAMMIE DODGERS

MAKES 10 BISCUITS

For the biscuits
200g/7oz/scant 1 cup cold butter, cubed
300g/10½oz/scant 2¼ cups plain
  (all-purpose) flour, plus extra for dusting
100g/3½oz/scant 1 cup icing (confectioners')
  sugar, sifted
1 egg yolk
½ tsp vanilla bean paste

For the filling
½ jar seeded raspberry jam or any other
  smooth jam you like
1 batch Vanilla Buttercream (see p.129)

These jammy biscuits are seriously good. The recipe is very simple, and by following a few tricks and tips in handling the sticky dough, the results will rock your world!

At the heart of my jammy biscuit is a gorgeous traditional Scottish shortbread biscuit recipe, which follows the '3-2-1' rule, where I mix 3 parts flour, to 2 parts butter, and 1 part sugar. I use icing sugar in my recipe rather than caster as I think it makes a really fine, smooth dough, which translates into a mouth-wateringly short, or crunchy biscuit after baking.

Small alphabet cutters aren't too tricky to buy online, but there are also plenty of creative alternatives to cut the centre out of your biscuit. I have found that a small shaped cutter, such as a heart, or a fine-pointed knife carefully used to cut a triangle shape, can give a great effect. You can even use the plastic part of a ballpoint pen (with the middle inky bit removed) to cut out small circles to represent polka dots, or eyes and a mouth to make a smiley face shape.

Put the butter and flour into a large bowl and, using your fingertips, crush the butter and flour together until it resembles fine breadcrumbs. Add the icing sugar and mix with a wooden spoon until it is just combined. When making shortbread or sugar cookies, overmixing the dough wakes the gluten up too much, and you will end up with puffy misshapen biscuits.

Add the egg yolk and vanilla and mix with the spoon until a smooth, fairly firm dough forms – it should be slightly sticky to the touch. If it is too crumbly, warm your hands and knead it gently in the bowl to heat up the butter and bring it all together.

Sandwich the dough between
2 sheets of clingfilm. Using a
rolling pin, roll it out until it is
about 2cm/¾in thick, then chill in
the refrigerator for at least 30 minutes.
Warning: skip this stage at your peril! Warm jammy dough is
extremely hard to work with!

Roll out the dough to just under ½cm/¼in thick on a heavily
floured work surface – this shortbread dough can be sticky, so
try to work quickly, keeping it as cool as possible. If you are new
to this, try rolling out smaller pieces of dough first, keeping the
rest in the refrigerator.

Using a fluted circle cutter, cut out as many rounds as you can.
Cut both 'fronts' and 'backs' for each biscuit. The fronts will
have the shapes cut out from the dough, and the backs will
be left plain. Using alphabet or shaped cutters, quickly and
carefully cut out a message or shape from the dough. Using a
palette knife, transfer the cut cookies to a baking tray lined with
parchment paper and chill again for 20 minutes.

Preheat the oven to 170°C/338°F/Gas mark 3.

Pop your cold baking tray directly into the hot oven and bake
for 7–10 minutes, or until the biscuits just start to turn golden
brown. Allow the cookies to cool before decorating.

To decorate, turn the jammy 'backs' onto their backs, so that
the 'inside' is exposed. Spread an even layer of jam in the
centre, making sure that once the 'front' is added, you will only
see jam through the message or shape.

Using a piping bag with a small tip cut off, pipe a round circle
of buttercream around the edge of the jammy to seal it and
prevent the jam from escaping!

Press the jammy 'fronts' onto the buttercream
for a second to seal, then chill in the refrigerator for
20 minutes until the buttercream sets hard then EAT!

These jammies will last for about 10 days if they are
kept in an airtight container.

PRETTY NICE BISCUITS

MAKES 10–15, DEPENDING ON CUTTER SIZE
90g/3¼oz/scant ½ cup butter, softened but not melted
50g/1¾oz/¼ cup caster (superfine) sugar,
    plus 1 tbsp for sprinkling
1 tsp vanilla extract
120g/4½oz/scant 1 cup plain (all-purpose) flour,
    plus extra for dusting
90g/3¼oz/1 cup desiccated (unsweetened shredded) coconut,
    finely chopped
1–3 tbsp cold water or milk
Gel paste food colourings of your choice

Whether you pronounce it nice, as in 'you have a nice dress' or 'neece', as in the French city, is a mere technicality – these biscuits are simply super-nice! Simple as you like to make, and easy to stamp words into as they hold their shape, they are a winner where I'm concerned. So roll out this recipe whenever you fancy a nice (or 'neece') old-fashioned treat.

Mix the butter, sugar and vanilla together in a large bowl with a wooden spoon until just combined. Add the flour and finely chopped desiccated coconut and continue mixing with the spoon, or your hands if you find that easier. At this stage, a dough should just about be coming together, so add 1 tablespoon water or milk at a time, until a stiff dough is formed. Add in your gel paste colours here, if you like, kneading gently to mix them through.

Squish the dough between 2 sheets of clingfilm and use a rolling pin to roll it out until it is about 2cm/¾in thick. Chill in the refrigerator for about 20 minutes to harden up.

Roll out the dough on a lightly floured surface until it is 1cm/½in thick. If the slab is too big for you to fit it onto your surface comfortably, roll out half at a time.

Cut out shapes of your choice and stamp or impress the letters or shapes that you like. I have snazzy alphabet stamps, but you can improvise by creating jagged capital letters with the flat end of a fork or spoon handle – write whatever word or message that takes your fancy. A nice touch is to add a border of dots around the edges by using the point of a cocktail stick or the end of a chopstick. Arrange the cut-out cookies on a baking tray lined with parchment paper. If you need your embossing impressions to come out of the oven really crisp, then chill the cookies in the refrigerator again for 10 minutes.

Preheat the oven to 175°C/347°F/Gas mark 4.

Dust the tops of the cookie lightly with sugar and bake in the oven for about 7–10 minutes, or until the edges of the cookies are just starting to turn golden brown. Get the kettle on and enjoy them while they are still warm!

DIGESTIVE BISCUITS

MAKES 8–10
75g/2¾oz/5 tbsp cold butter, cut into pieces
100g/3½oz/¾ cup wholemeal plain (whole-wheat) flour,
  plus extra for dusting
65g/2¼oz/¾ cup fine or medium oatmeal
¼ tsp bicarbonate of soda (baking soda)
35g/1¼oz/2 heaping tbsp soft brown sugar
1–2 tbsp milk
melted chocolate or coloured flood Royal Icing
  (pp.132–135) for dipping (optional)

Put the butter, flour and oatmeal into a large bowl and, using your fingertips, crush the ingredients together until it is a breadcrumb-like consistency. Add the bicarbonate of soda and sugar and mix briefly to combine. Add 1 tbsp milk and, using your hands, try to bring the mixture together to form a dough. You may need to add a little more milk to bring it together into 1 big lump – you are looking for a dough that sticks together, but doesn't stick all over your hands.

Squidge and squeeze the dough into a thick slab, and sandwich it between 2 sheets of clingfilm. Use a rolling pin to roll it out to about 2cm/¾in thick, then chill the dough in the refrigerator for at least 30 minutes to harden up.

Line a baking sheet with parchment paper.

When the dough is cold, roll it out on a floured surface to about 1cm/½in thick. If you're a new to this, try rolling one-third of your dough out first, keeping the rest in the refrigerator, as it will be an easier amount to handle.

Using a straight-edged cookie cutter, or the rim of a small mug or glass, carefully cut out as many rounds as you can from the dough and pop them onto the lined baking tray, then chill in the refrigerator for 20 minutes.

Preheat the oven to 170°C/338°F/Gas mark 3.

Emboss some of the tops if you like – I used the blunt side of a butter knife, the barrel of a pen that I had removed the inky bit from, a clean spatula, and the wire rack from my kitchen to press shapes into the dough – try for a few different shapes if you can.

Bake the cookies in the oven for about 10–12 minutes, or until the edges are just starting to turn golden brown. Allow to cool on a wire rack.

If you like, you can dip some of your biscuits into melted chocolate or coloured royal icing, or just enjoy with a nice cup of tea!

STENCILLED COOKIES

MAKES AS MANY AS YOU WOULD LIKE

Alphabet or number stencils of your choice
(use the ones at the back of the book, or
you can make your own stencils by cutting
carefully into a sheet of acetate or card
with a craft knife. You can also buy certain
standard shapes online or in crafting shops)

1 batch cookies of your choice, iced with
sugarpaste icing (ready-to-roll/fondant
icing) (I used chocolate sugar cookie dough
iced in bright colours. Allow the icing to set
hard before use)

Gel paste food colourings of your choosing

a small sponge (clean unused make-up ones
are good)

Lettering, typography and fonts in food art and installations
always look so awesome to me that I had to include this recipe
for stencilled cookies. I was given a beautiful book full of
amazing font and lettering stencils called *The Alphabet Stencil
Book* and have used their stencils for these. Or you could use
the stencils provided at the back of this book.

Stencilling with gel paste colours often takes a few tries to get
the perfect finish, so have a practice on a piece of paper to test
your technique first.

Place your stencil over the top of your iced cookie and hold
steady. Using your sponge dabbed gently into the paste, sponge
the colour across the stencil onto the icing underneath, making
sure it goes into every nook and cranny of the stencil.

Lift the stencil away gently but with steady hands and ensure it
doesn't drag across the cookies, as this will leave marks.

Tidy up any messy edges with a piece of kitchen paper or
the point of a sharp knife and allow to dry before serving
or packaging up.

TRASH CAN COOKIES

MAKES 8–12

220g/7¾oz plain (semisweet)
  chocolate
30g/1oz/2 tbsp salted butter,
  cut into pieces
2 eggs
65g/2¼oz/¼ cup + 2 tbsp soft
  brown sugar
65g/2¼oz/¼ cup + 2 tbsp
  caster (superfine) sugar
½ tsp vanilla extract
40g/1½oz/¼ cup plain
  (all-purpose) flour
¼ tsp baking powder

1 tsp ground coffee (the sort you'd put into a caffetière)
5 very small handfuls of any 5 of the below:
  salted ridged crisps (potato chips)
  chopped dates or prunes
  raisins, currants or sultanas (golden raisins)
  spicy peanuts or regular nuts chopped into large chunks
  pine nuts
  pumpkin seeds
  banana chips
  pretzels
  chocolate chips
  1 big tsp any type of nut butter
  1 tbsp sesame seeds or poppy seeds or pumpkin seeds

This recipe is the biscuit BOSS! Yes, they have a bit of an attention-seeking title, but they are actually pretty delicious, and play on the whole 'sweet and savoury' thing. You don't actually need to raid the bin (DUH), but they are the perfect way to use up all those random ingredients in the back of your cupboard. Have fun with them, and my tip is to always include the plain crisps... they are the best!

Melt the chocolate and butter together in a heatproof bowl set over a pan of gently simmering water, making sure the bottom of the bowl doesn't touch the water. Remove from the heat as soon as it has melted and formed a thick gooey paste. Wait for it to cool slightly before mixing with the other ingredients.

In a separate bowl, whisk the eggs, sugars and vanilla together until the mixture is full of bubbles and lighter in colour. This should take about 5 minutes if you are using your baking biceps, or about 1 minute if you are cheating with a food mixer!

Combine the chocolate and egg mixtures together in a large bowl then add the flour, baking powder and coffee and mix until smooth.

Preheat the oven to 170°C/338°F/Gas mark 3 and line a baking sheet with parchment paper.

Add your 5 small handfuls of goodies into the bowl and mix until combined. Using 2 dessertspoons, drop equally sized dollops onto the lined baking sheet, keeping them about 5cm/2in apart as they will spread a little when baking. Aim for a small round cookie and heap the mixture in the middle a little.

Bake the cookies in the oven for 10–12 minutes. Remove them just when the edges are just starting to crisp up – this way it will ensure that you have a lovely gooey cookie in the middle. Allow to cool on the sheet.

SWEET BREADSTICKS

MAKES ABOUT 40 COOKIE STICKS

60g/2¼oz/¼ cup butter, softened but not melted
50g/1¾oz/¼ cup caster (superfine) sugar
1 egg
½ tsp vanilla bean extract
120g/4½oz/generous ¾ cup strong bread flour
   or pasta flour ('00' type)
2–3 tbsp cold water
100g/3½oz milk or white chocolate, for dipping
   (tint it with oil-based food colourings if you like)
sprinkles or finely chopped nuts to decorate (optional)

'Pocky' sweet breadsticks were first sold by a Japanese company in 1966, under the strapline 'the snack with a handle'. It's a brilliant and simple idea really – make a crispy sweet breadstick and dunk it in chocolate. They are great fun and make really cute party favours or sweet canapés, so give them a try.

In a large bowl, mix the butter and sugar together with a wooden spoon until it is just creamed. Add the egg and vanilla and mix again, then add the flour and beat for about 5 minutes until the mixture resembles a smooth elastic paste. This long mix will wake up the gluten and give you a nice firm biscuit when baked. You want the paste to hold its shape when piped, so practice making ribbons in the bowl. You need them to keep their shape and not sink into the mixture. If your mix isn't thick enough add a little more flour.

Spoon the mixture into a piping bag fitted with a nozzle about 6–8mm/⅜in across. You can use a freezer bag, but it's trickier to get perfect circles, which is what you are looking for.

Preheat the oven 160°C/325°F/Gas mark 3 and line a baking tray with parchment paper.

Pipe straight lines about 12–15cm/4½–6in long onto the lined tray. Do this by touching the piping nozzle to the parchment and squeezing gently as you pull the bag slowly towards yourself keeping a 2cm/¾in height from the parchment. If it takes you a couple of tries to get this technique right, just scoop up the first few lines and pop them back into the bag! You only need to leave a little space between lines as they don't spread when baking.

Bake in the oven for about 5–7 minutes, checking after 5 minutes. They are done when there's just the tiniest hint of colour on the tops. Allow to cool.

Melt the chocolate in a heatproof bowl set over a pan of gently simmering water, making sure the bottom of the bowl doesn't touch the water.

Dip the cooled cookies into the melted chocolate about three-quarters of the way in, using a teaspoon to help pour the chocolate on top if you need to. Place the cookies back onto the lined baking tray and add a sprinkling of chopped nuts or colourful sprinkles if you like. Allow to set. They will last a week if you keep them in an airtight container.

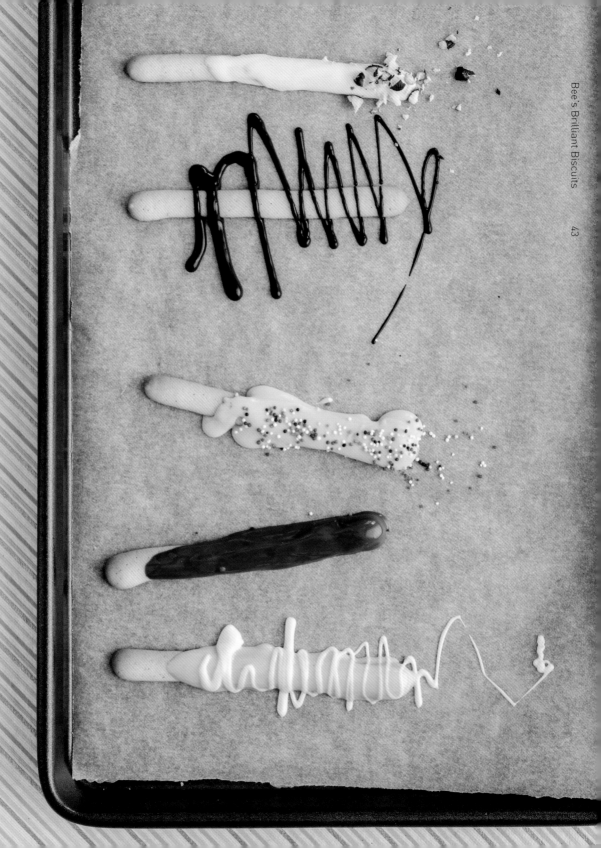

FUNNY FACES

These cookies are perfect for making with kids as they can help dip the cookies into the chocolate to make the 'hair'. The recipe is great for using up any scraps of dough that you have left in the freezer, and works with most basic dough recipes.

Line a baking tray with parchment paper.

Roll out as many medium-sized rounds of dough as you like. The more different types you use the better. If you are baking these cookies from freezer scraps, defrost the dough by leaving out on a work surface for about 30 minutes before rolling.

Using a teaspoon, a blunt knife and any other cutlery that makes a shape you like, make a selection of impressions on the dough to create a range of smiley faces. You can be creative here – try a cheeky angled smile, or different shapes created with the handle end of a teaspoon for the nose. Chopstick tips make great little eyes and the edge of a bigger spoon can depict a hat or fringe!

Once you have made all the impressions you like, put the cookies onto the lined baking tray and chill in the refrigerator for at least 30 minutes.

MAKES ABOUT 15–20 COOKIES
approximately 1 batch Go-to Shortbread
  dough (p.19), Gingerbread dough (p.74),
  Classic Vanilla Sugar Cookie dough (p.18),
  or scraps from other dough that you
  have stored in the freezer and defrosted
  before use
200g/7oz milk chocolate
100g/3½oz white chocolate
  (add ½ tsp ground tea leaves to
  create grey hair)

Preheat the oven to 175°C/347°F/Gas mark 4.

Pop your cold baking tray directly into the hot oven and bake in the oven for about 7–10 minutes, removing any cookies that are done earlier with a palette knife and allowing the others to continue baking. Allow to cool on a wire rack or clean work surface.

Meanwhile, melt the chocolate, by putting the different types in 2 separate heatproof bowls set over a pan of gently simmering water, making sure the bottoms of the bowls don't touch the water.

When the cookies are cool, dip the sides of the hair first, then the top and shake off any excess chocolate before laying them down to set on a clean sheet of parchment. Try to get a different range of hairstyles, from full coverage, to a centre parting, and do some grey hair too. If you are dipping in the white chocolate to get a beard effect, you may need to re-score the mouth impression to make sure it can be seen clearly. Add sprinkles or chocolate shavings and allow the chocolate on your cookies to set before eating. Enjoy!

PARTY RINGS

MAKES ABOUT 14–16 PARTY RING COOKIES
1 batch of your favourite cookie dough,
   chilled for 30 minutes:
      Classic Vanilla Sugar Cookie dough (p.18), Salt and Pepper
      Chocolate Cookie dough (p.80), Speculoos (p.77) and my
      Go-to Shortbread dough (see p.19) all work well
1 batch soft peak Royal Icing (p.132)
as many gel paste colours as you like
   (I use bright yellow, hot pink, mint green, blue and white)

These cookies make me feel really nostalgic – I remember having them in my packed lunch at school. Now I'm grown-up, I make my own neon versions!

Roll out the cookie dough until it is about 1cm/½in thick, and using 2 circular, square or hexagonal cookie cutters, cut out as many doughnut-shaped cookies as you can from the dough, then place them onto a baking tray lined with parchment paper. Chill in the refrigerator for 15 minutes.

Preheat the oven to 170°C/344°F/Gas mark 3.

Meanwhile, prepare enough icing for the rings by mixing the various paste colours into dollops of soft peak royal icing and adding a few drops of water until you get a runnier flood consistency that ribbons for between 5–10 seconds. Remember to place a wet jiffy cloth over the top of your icing to stop it going hard.

For each cookie you need:
• Enough flood icing in white to cover the top of each biscuit.
• Enough contrasting coloured icing to pipe several lines across the top of each cookie.

Pop your cold baking tray directly into the hot oven and bake in the oven for about 10–12 minutes according to size. Allow to cool on a wire rack or clean work surface.

Spread the white icing on top of your cookie with a little palette knife or piping bag, aiming for a thickness of about 2–3mm/¹⁄₁₆–¹⁄₈in, then pipe some irregular lines of the contrast coloured icing on top. Either leave as clean crisp lines, or drag a cocktail stick across the surface of the biscuit to create a cool dogtooth effect.

Allow to dry completely before eating – ideally overnight, or speed this drying process up by popping your cookies into an oven preheated to 50°C/122°F/lowest possible Gas mark for about 15 minutes.

ICED GEMS

MAKES ABOUT 40–50 ICED GEMS
1 batch Salt and Pepper Chocolate Cookie dough (p.80),
  chilled for 30 minutes
as many gel paste colours as you like (I use bright yellow,
  orange, hot pink, green and turquoise)
1 batch stiff peak Royal Icing (p.132)
edible glitter, for dusting (optional)

These rock, and make brilliant presents. You can also use them to decorate a birthday cake!

Line a baking tray with parchment paper.

Roll out the chocolate cookie dough until it is about 1cm/½in thick. Using the smallest cutter you have, ideally about 2cm/¾in across, cut out as many little circles or other shapes as you can and put them these onto the lined baking tray. Chill in the refrigerator for 15 minutes.

Preheat the oven to 160°C/325°F/Gas mark 3.

Meanwhile, prepare enough icing for your gems by mixing the paste colour into a dollop of stiff peak royal icing, remembering to place a wet jiffy cloth over the top of your icing to stop it going hard.

Pop your cold baking tray directly into the hot oven and bake for about 5–7 minutes according to size. Allow to cool on a wire rack or clean work surface.

Preheat the oven to 50°C/122°F/lowest possible Gas mark.

Pop a medium or large (depending on the size of your cookie) closed star nozzle into a piping bag and spoon your coloured royal icing into it. Line the baking tray with fresh parchment paper and begin to pipe little gem shapes on top, keeping them quite close together.

Hold your piping bag totally vertical, and with your dominant hand leading the way, touch your piping tip to the parchment and squeeze while pulling away slowly. When you have most of the shape piped, stop squeezing and pull away gently – this should leave you with a nice peak of icing. Have a little practice run to get your shapes right and a sense check to make sure that you're piping the right size, and repeat until you have enough tops for all of your cookies.

Pop the icing gems into the cool oven for about 25 minutes, and you will find that this speeds up the drying process.

When you are ready to put them on top of the cookies, just use a tiny little dot of any leftover icing to stick them in place. You can also dust them with edible glitter for a lovely sparkly finish.

THE ULTIMATE GOOEY CHOCOLATE COOKIES

MAKES 10–12 MEDIUM-SIZED COOKIES
220g/8oz plain (semisweet) chocolate, broken into pieces
30g/1oz/2 tbsp salted butter
2 eggs
110g/4oz/½ cup granulated sugar
½ tsp vanilla bean paste
45g/1½oz/⅓ cup plain (all-purpose) flour
¼ tsp baking powder
60g/2¼oz/½ cup fresh raspberries, dried cherries, pecans or
    hazelnuts (optional)

Let's be clear – this gooey chocolate cookie is the MOTHER of all chocolate cookies. It's seriously rich, soft and gooey in the middle, with a lovely crisp and shiny surface. These are ridiculously delicious and they are guaranteed to help you win friends and influence people – they are simply the ultimate chocolate cookies.

Preheat the oven to 175°C/347°F/Gas mark 4 and line a baking tray with parchment paper.

Melt the chocolate and butter together in a heatproof bowl set over a pan of gently simmering water, making sure the bottom of the bowl doesn't touch the water. Remove from the heat and allow to cool.

Meanwhile, whisk the eggs, sugar and vanilla together in another bowl for about 5 minutes until they are lighter in colour and frothy.

When the chocolate mixture has cooled down a little, scoop it into the sugar, egg and vanilla mixture, folding it in gently until combined. Add the flour and baking powder along with the fruit or nuts and mix until you have a nice smooth consistently coloured mixture – it will be thick and gloopy.

Using 2 dessertspoons or an ice-cream scoop, drop regularly sized and shaped dollops of mixture onto the lined baking tray, leaving about 4cm/1½in in between each cookie as they will spread a little when baking. Try to make your dollops small, round and with a bit of height. Bake in the oven for 10–12 minutes then allow to cool on the tray before peeling off the parchment paper and devouring these mighty beasts!

Serving suggestion: These cookies make amazing ice-cream sandwiches, and can be layered easily to make a Birthday Cookie Cake (see p.52).

BIRTHDAY COOKIE CAKE

MAKES A 13CM/5IN ROUND, FIVE-LAYER BIRTHDAY CAKE
2 batches Ultimate Chocolate Cookie Dough (p.51)
1 batch Vanilla Buttercream (p.129), coloured if you like
candles, flags, sparkers or any other decoration as you like,
  to decorate

Layer cakes are one thing, but a layered cookie cake is a whole different animal! This cookie cake has enough wow factor to make you extremely popular at any party, so have a bit of fun with the decorations and create something beautiful!

Preheat the oven to 170°C/338°F/Gas mark 3 and line 2 baking trays with parchment paper.

Prepare a double batch of the Ultimate Chocolate Cookie Dough according to the instructions on p.51. Using a pencil, draw five 13cm/5in round circles onto the lined baking trays, leaving about 5cm/2in between each one. Use a bowl or plate to draw around if you can find one that's about the right size.

Spoon a large dollop of the cookie dough into the middle of each circle and spread to the edges carefully. Make sure you have approximately the same amount of cookie batter in each circle, so that your cookies are roughly the same size and height.

Bake the cookies in the oven for about 15–18 minutes, making sure that they come out of the oven nice and gooey. Allow to cool.

Meanwhile, prepare a batch of Vanilla Buttercream according to the instructions on p.129. Split and colour the batch in as many colours as you like. Two colours are good for a stripy effect, or deepening shades of the same colour create an ombré effect, as here.

When the cookies are cool, set the prettiest, most even cookie aside, this will be your top cookie.

For the others, spread a layer of buttercream on the tops, paying attention to your spreading at the edges – use a spoon or palette to create a nice pretty edge. Pop these cookies into the refrigerator for 15 minutes to firm up the icing and make sure that it doesn't all squish out when you assemble the cookie cake.

Stack up the cookie cake, picking the prettiest most uniform section as your front, and add candles, flags, sparklers or other decorations as you like. Keep cool until serving and use a very sharp knife to cut slices.

KAPOW! SUPERHERO COOKIES

MAKES 10 COOKIES
1 slab sugarpaste icing (ready-to-roll/fondant icing),
   cut into 3 fist-sized chunks
paste colours, I used yellow and red
icing (confectioners') sugar, for dusting
1 batch of your favourite cookie dough cut out and baked
   into rounds or speech bubble shapes. I used Vanilla Sugar
   Cookie dough (p.18)
1 black edible ink marker pen

Superheroes get the coolest words – POW, BAM, KRUNCH! The bright bold colours and jagged shapes really lend themselves to the type of cookies I like best; graphic bold ones.

These cookie toppers are very easy to make, you just need to find a good strong edible ink marker pen from cake decorating shops or online and then you are set! These would make excellent party favours.

Colour 2 fist-sized chunks of sugarpaste icing in bright yellow and red, keeping some white separately. Roll out the red sugarpaste to less than 5mm/¼in if you can on a surface dusted with icing sugar, and cut out as many of your chosen cookie shapes as you need – I made little circles and speech bubble shapes.

Brush the tops of the baked and cooled cookies with a little water and stick the red sugarpaste icing on top. Roll out the white icing as thinly as possible and cut out a shape that's just smaller than the red shape. Again stick this on with a little water. Use the edible ink pen to dot the top with a mixture of regularly shaped

polka dots and stripes. Remember that you only need to draw on the pieces of icing that will be seen once the POW banner is on top, so focus on the edges and don't waste your ink on the middles!

Roll out the yellow icing and, using a small sharp knife, cut out a jagged edged shape. If you are finding it hard to get an even shape, then cut out a template from card that fits on the top of the cookie and use this as a guide.

Use the edible pen to write a bold selection of words in the middle. You can be as creative as you like here but standard classics that work are POW, BAM, KAPOW, SPLAT, KRUNCH, BOOM and ZAM.

Allow the icing to dry for 1 hour at room temperature. You can speed up the drying process by popping the piped cookies into a 50°C/122°F/lowest possible Gas mark oven for about 20 minutes before serving or packaging.

BEETROOT AND CREAM CHEESE WHOOPIE PIES

MAKES 12–15 WHOOPIE PIES, DEPENDING ON THE SIZE

For the whoopie pies
110g/4oz/½ cup butter, softened but not melted
180g/6oz/scant 1 cup soft brown sugar
1 egg
220g/8oz/1½ cups self-raising flour
20g/¾oz/scant ¼ cup cocoa powder
120g/4½oz cooked beetroot, finely grated
a large pinch of salt and a grind of black pepper
125ml/4fl oz/½ cup sour cream
For the filling
250g/9oz tub of cream cheese
salt and freshly ground black pepper

These unusual savoury cake-like cookies are inspired by some delicious beetroot macarons filled with goat's cheese that a fantastic chef and my old kitchen buddy Paul used to make. Beetroot adds a delicate, earthy flavour and texture to cookies and cakes, and the colour in these is pretty – they make a really interesting canapé.

Preheat the oven to 175°C/347°F/Gas mark 4 and line a baking tray with parchment paper.

For the filling, put the cream cheese into a bowl, season with salt and pepper and beat until it is light and fluffy. Cover and set aside.

For the whoopee pies, in a large bowl, mix the butter and sugar vigorously until it's light and fluffy and pale in colour. Add the egg and mix again until combined, then mix in the flour and

cocoa powder, and finally the beetroot, salt and pepper and sour cream. You will have a smooth paste, similar to a cake batter rather than a cookie dough.

Using 2 teaspoons or a piping bag, drop regularly sized domed circles of the cookie mixture about 5cm/2in in diameter onto the lined tray, leaving a little space in between each one as they will spread during baking. Bake in the oven for 8–10 minutes, checking at 8 minutes to see if they're done by pressing on the top – if they bounce back then they are good to go but don't wait until the edges start to colour.

Allow to cool, then when cold, smudge a generous small dollop of the cream cheese into the middle of half of the pieces, and press another whoopee pie on top to seal. Eat!

BROKEN BISCUIT BARK

MAKES BETWEEN 18–20 PIECES,
  DEPENDING ON HOW BIG YOU CUT THEM
125g/4½oz/½ cup butter
200g/7oz plain (semisweet) or milk chocolate
150g/5½oz white chocolate
100g/3½oz bashed up, ugly or broken biscuits (cookies), any
  type at all (I used gingerbread and vanilla)
edible glitter or sprinkles, to decorate (optional)

Biscuits break, fact! They get crushed by accident, a bit misshapen and ugly during baking, or are just surplus to requirements, but that's no excuse the bin them – store them in a freezerproof bag and freeze them with other cookie rejects, then use at a later date.

This is a lush recipe that's easy to adapt and make your own, and better still, it's technically recycling, so you can feel good about it too!

Line a baking tray with parchment paper.

Gently melt the plain chocolate in a bowl set over a pan of gently simmering water.

Meanwhile, smash up the broken biscuits with your hands or a rolling pin until there are a range of different sized pieces, from sandy crumbs through to some crunchier nuggets. Throw these biscuit pieces into the pan with the chocolate and stir until combined.

Pour this gloopy mixture into the prepared baking tray and press the surface down with the back of a spoon to crush everything together and smooth out. Chill in the refrigerator for at least 2 hours.

Melt your white chocolate in the same way as before. Allow to cool slightly, before pouring it over the top of your chilled mixture. While the chocolate is still a little warm, add your sprinkles or glitter to the top.

Place back in the fridge to cool right down. If you'd like to create shards, use a sharp blunt object, such as the end of a rolling pin, to smash into portion-sized pieces and enjoy!

NANKHATAI INDIAN SHORTBREAD

MAKES 10–20 COOKIES DEPENDING ON SIZE
110g/4oz/½ cup cold butter, cut into pieces
175g/6oz/1¼ cups plain (all-purpose) flour or a mixture of rice or gram flour and plain (all-purpose) flour, plus extra for dusting
75g/2¾oz/scant ⅔ cup icing (confectioners') sugar

2 tsp dried rose petals (available from large supermarkets or Indian and Iranian supermarkets), roughly chopped, plus extra for decorating
4 cardamom pods, seeds removed and finely crushed
1½ tsp rose water

We all know about fusion cuisine, but what about fusion baking, like this recipe for a Scottish/Indian shortbread?

The name is a fusion of two cultures too – nankhatai is a combination of the Persian word 'nan' (meaning bread) with 'khatai', which in northeast Iran and Afghanistan is a type of biscuit. These cookies are subtly flavoured with cardamom and rose petals without being spicy at all, and they are brilliant served with a nice strong cuppa – or even a mug of chai tea.

Line a baking tray with parchment paper.

Put the butter and flour into a large bowl and use your fingertips to crush the butter into the flour until it resembles breadcrumbs. Add the icing sugar, rose petals and cardamom then combine with your hands until the dough starts to come together. Pour in the rose water and combine until a firm dough is formed, but don't work it too much.

Roll out the dough on a lightly floured surface until it is 2cm/¾in thick. Cut the dough into regular shapes, either with a fluted circular cookie cutter, or with the rim of a small mug or glass. Arrange the cookies on the lined baking tray, about 4cm/1½in apart and chill in the refrigerator for about 20 minutes, or until cold and firm.

Preheat the oven to 170°C/338°F/Gas mark 3.

Pop your cold baking tray directly into the hot oven and bake for 20 minutes, or until golden brown on the edges. Allow to cool. Decorate with a few extra dried rose petals and serve warm with a good strong cup of chai!

Nankhatai pictured here with Rangoli Piped Cookies (p.62).

RANGOLI PIPED COOKIES

MAKES AS MANY AS YOU WOULD LIKE
Batches of any basic cookie recipe, cut into your preferred shapes
  (I use the Classic Vanilla Sugar Cookie recipe on p.18)
sugarpaste (ready-to-roll/fondant) icing,
  coloured with paste colours
1 batch of soft peak Royal Icing (see p.134),
  coloured with paste colours
an edible ink pen (optional)
gold lustre (optional)
piping gel or alcohol (optional)

I first noticed Rangoli patterns when I was travelling through India a few years ago, and loved seeing women making the bright vibrant patterns on their doorsteps using coloured flour, sand, rice and even petals during Diwali, the Indian festival of light. Certain designs are said to bring good luck. I think the patterns are beautiful and love their intricacy and detail. I've enjoyed making these for my buddy Dimple and her family for Diwali. See image on p.61.

First, make up your cookies in your preferred shapes and ice with sugarpaste icing.

Mix up several different colours of soft peak consistency Royal Icing according to the instruction on p.134, and pop a big spoonful of each into a piping bag with a fine nozzle. I used a 1.5 and a 1 PME nozzle for these. It's very tricky to get the detailed effect without a professional piping bag and nozzle, so use one if you can.

I find it helpful to trace the main outlines of the piping detail onto the surface of the cookie before I pipe it and you can do this with an edible pen, a scribe tool or cocktail stick.

Tie the top of your piping bag and make sure it is not overfilled as this will make it tricky to handle. Squeeze gently and with a consistent pressure with your dominant hand. Use the index finger of your other hand to help guide the piping nozzle – this will make for a smoother piped line. Once piped, think about highlighting any focal points with a light dusting of gold lustre dust mixed in with a small amount of piping gel, alcohol or water to make a paste.

If you are using more than one colour and layering or piping two colours right next to each other, let the first one set on a wire rack before piping the next one to avoid the colours bleeding into each other. You can speed up the drying process by popping the piped cookies into an oven preheated to 50°C/122°F/lowest possible Gas mark for about 20 minutes.

Tip
I find it tricky to create patterns this pretty without having something to take inspiration from. Luckily it is very easy to find patterns on Pinterest! Think carefully about your patterns and colours before you start.

MINI WEDDING COOKIE CAKES

I love these dinky little cookie cakes, perfect for edible wedding favours and pretty versatile too – you can use lots of different types of dough, and they are easy to decorate in a number of different ways.

Cut and bake 3 cookies of each size (small, medium and large) to form the base units of the cookie cake. My cookies were 7cm/2¾in, 5cm/2in and 3cm/1¼in rounds. Allow to cool.

When your cookies are cool, decorate in your preferred style – you can rough ice them with dollops of royal icing, fill them to resemble a layer cake, or use thin layers of coloured sugarpaste, as I did here. Consider making some little sugarpaste flowers, or use sprinkles and edible glitter to jazz them up, whatever takes your fancy.

MAKES 5 X THREE-TIER COOKIE CAKES
1 batch of your favourite cookie dough
  (I use Vanilla Sugar Cookie Dough, p.18)
Sugarpaste (ready-to-roll/fondant) icing,
  coloured using gel paste colours,
1 batch soft peak Royal Icing in your preferred
  colour (p.132)
sprinkles or edible glitter, to decorate
  (optional)

Layer up your cookies using a little spot of royal icing in between each one to secure them in place. You can package them in little boxes or cellophane bags, tied with a pretty ribbon.

CHOCOLATE CHIP WEDDING CAKE

I have the pleasure of baking countless wedding cakes at Bee's Bakery, but especially love making cookie cakes. This chocolate chip dough is remarkably adaptable, and if you ever so slightly underbake it inside a cake tin, it makes a lovely regularly shaped cookie cake – I have used some fresh edible flowers to decorate this cake, and I think it looks pretty damn stunning!

Preheat the oven to 175°C/347°F/Gas mark 4 and line your baking tins with parchment paper – you will need one 10cm/4in tin, one 15cm/6in and one 20cm/8in tin.

Mix the flour and baking powder together and set aside.

In a large bowl, combine the butter and sugar vigorously until it is light and fluffy – using a food mixer for this will save a lot of energy! Add the vanilla extract and eggs and mix until combined. Add the flour in 2 batches, mixing between additions, then add the chocolate chips and mix until a smooth dough is formed with the chips equally distributed throughout.

Pour about 4–5cm/1½–2in deep of mixture into each of the lined tins, spreading the mixture evenly over the bottom of the tin, and making a little well in the middle of the mixture so that the centre doesn't rise ridiculously high when it is baked. This should use up about a third of the mixture.

MAKES 1 THREE-TIERED COOKIE CAKE, TIERS MEASURE 20CM/8IN, 15CM/6IN AND 10CM/4IN

810g/1lb 12oz/5¾ cups plain (all-purpose) flour
1½ tsp baking powder
690g/1lb 8oz/3 cups butter, softened
780g/1lb 11oz/4 cups caster (superfine) or soft brown sugar
6 tsp vanilla extract
6 eggs
500–700g/1lb 2oz–1lb 9oz/scant 3–4 cups chocolate chips, to taste
2 batches Vanilla Buttercream (p.129)
edible flower petals, coloured buttercream or sprinkles, to decorate

Bake for about 10 minutes for the smallest tin, 15 minutes for the middle one and up to 25 minutes for the bigger tin. If the mixture is slightly undercooked in the middle this isn't a problem. Remove from the oven, carefully remove the cookies from the tins and allow to cool on a wire rack. If creating a larger cake, repeat the baking process until you have three cookie layers for each tier.

When all your giant cookie pieces are baked and cooled, trim the tops if needed to make sure that each of your layers is about the same height. Spread a generous layer of buttercream in between each layer and allow to chill in the refrigerator before adding the next layer – this will prevent your buttercream from squidging out of the sides when you stack them up.

Decorate with edible flower petals, or consider using coloured buttercream or sprinkles for a fun finish. When you cut the cake, cut into squares by following a grid pattern, rather than slices.

MUG OF TEA COOKIE

MAKES 4–5 DEPENDING ON SIZE
1 batch Vanilla Sugar Cookie dough (p.18)
2 tsp good-quality teabag contents or finely ground tea leaves
butter, for greasing
plain (all-purpose) flour, for dusting
150g/5½oz plain (semisweet) or milk chocolate, broken into small pieces, for lining the mug
1 batch Royal Icing (p.132)
a mug of chilled tea, either iced fruit tea, cold brew tea (leave your teabag in a mug of cold water overnight then add milk and/or sugar to taste), or iced coffee also works

You will also need:
The bottom part of a metal cocktail shaker or an oven-safe mug, e.g. enamel
Baking beads
  (or uncooked rice/lentils)

Who wants to have their cup of tea and eat it?! My mate Joe Kinch has a tea company called Joe's Tea, and they make the best tea I have ever tasted. This is one of the coolest little cookie constructions I have ever made, so have a go and be the boss of afternoon tea... just like Joe!

Line a baking tray with parchment paper.

Make the dough according to the method on p.18, adding the 2 teaspoons loose tea together with the vanilla and egg. Chill in the refrigerator for 30 minutes.

Generously grease the inside of the cocktail shaker or mug at least two-thirds the way up with butter.

Once your dough is chilled, roll out a long rectangular shape on a lightly floured surface to about 7–8 mm/¼in thick. Cut out a round disc the same size as the inside of the base of the cocktail shaker or mug – this needs to fit snugly but evenly inside, so push it down all the way to the bottom.

Using the mug as a guide, cut a long thin strip about 10–12cm/4–4½in tall from the dough, this will form the walls of your mug. The strip needs to be long enough to fit all the way around the inside of the shaker or mug so start long and trim it once you know it definitely fits.

Carefully roll the strip of dough up into a spiral, like a carpet, and insert it into the mug, pressing down so the bottom edge connects with the disc in the bottom.

Using your fingertips, carefully unravel the coil of dough, making sure that the edges are even, and that the bottom disc is sealed in place. Smooth out any lumps or bumps with your fingers then cut the dough with a sharp knife at the point that the 2 ends start to overlap. Make sure that the join between the 2 edges of dough is squished together.

Make a mug handle or two out of all the dough trimmings. Try a couple of different designs, one big and one smaller, so you have a choice once they are baked. Set aside on the lined baking tray.

Next, push a large piece of clingfilm a little way down inside the dough-lined mould. Add some baking beans, uncooked rice or lentils, pushing them down to make sure that the cookie dough stays mug shaped while it is baking. Without these, the cookie will collapse. Gather the top of the clingfilm up around the beans to seal it and chill or, better still, freeze it for 20 minutes. Chill or freeze the handles as well.

Preheat the oven to 175°C/347°F/Gas mark 4.

Bake the mould, including the beans, for 10–12 minutes until the top of the mug is starting to brown. Carefully remove the bean package, and bake for another 5 minutes to seal the dough inside. Bake the handles at the same time for about 7–10 minutes.

Cool the cookie in the mug on a wire rack for about 10 minutes, then, once it is at room temperature, gently tap the cookie out. Allow the handles to cool.

Attach the cooled handles to the body of the cooled mug with a generous dot of royal icing.

Melt the chocolate in a heatproof bowl set over a pan of gently simmering water, making sure the bottom of the bowl doesn't touch the water. Pour 2–3 tablespoons of the melted chocolate into the mug and turn it this way and that until a good solid seal is made on the inside – this needs to be water (or tea) tight. You can use a pastry brush dipped in the chocolate to seal any gaps, if you need to. Allow to cool.

When cool, pour yourself a nice cup of chilled tea, and enjoy! Don't hold your full mug just by the handle, as it may not be strong enough to support the weight! Store in an airtight container for up to a week.

SPECKLED EASTER COOKIES

This speckled effect is simple to achieve and very pretty, so don't give eggs for Easter, try cookies instead! I cut my cookies into egg shapes with some old metal circle cutters bent into an oval shape, but you might find it easier to make a card template and cut around it!

MAKES 10–14 COOKIES

1 batch of your favourite cookie dough, baked, cooled and iced with sugarpaste (ready-to-roll/fondant) icing, coloured with paste colours

1–2 tbsp cocoa powder

Arrange the iced cookies on a large piece of parchment paper to protect your work surface and walls. Put 1 heaped tablespoon cocoa powder into a mug and mix in enough cold water to make a very thick paste, like custard.

Dip a pastry brush into the paste and gently flick the bristles with a finger in the direction you want speckles to appear. Have a test first to get your technique right! Speckle randomly and wildly across all the cookies and allow to dry for 1 hour, before serving or packaging up.

COOKIE HOUSES

What I love best about small houses like these is how easy it is to make your own mark on them, so try adding some details that personalise your house. Try icing the name or number of the house you are making, or bake a little tiny dog or cat shaped cookie if that fits the bill.

MAKES 3–4 HOUSES

Per house

1 batch dough (I used Gingerbread Cookie dough (see p.74) for the winter house and Classic Vanilla Sugar Cookie dough (see p.18) for the beach house)

plain (all-purpose) flour, for dusting

Sugarpaste (ready-to-roll/fondant) icing, coloured using paste colours of your choosing (used on beach houses)

1 batch Royal Icing (see p.132)

sprinkles and other props of your choosing to jazz up your icing

To create a cookie house that's about 12cm/4½in tall, you will need one set of the below pieces per house. Making cardboard templates by cutting up a cereal box always helps me.

For the cookie house components

2 roof pieces at 8 x 5cm/3¼ x 2in each

2 side pieces at 7 x 4.5cm/2¾ x 1¾in each

2 more side pieces, which will form the front and back – as above measurements, with a slanted end that the roof will sit on cut at 4.5cm/1¾in tall along the long edge, to the top of the piece – see the pic to guide you. Remember to cut a front door out of the middle

1 base piece to stand the gingerbread house on – this can be round or square but must be about 12–14cm/4½–5½in across

Any other pieces you like – a front door, and try cutting a mini tree, or a snowman shape or a sandcastle

COOKIE HOUSES (CONTINUED)

Line 2 baking sheets with parchment paper.

Roll our your dough carefully and evenly on a floured surface to ½cm/¼in thick maximum – any thicker and it won't keep its shape when it is baking. Cut out as many pieces as you can from the dough, including a few spare pieces in case of any breakages in the baking and/or decorating process.

Transfer the cut cookies onto the lined baking sheet remembering to put any smaller ones on a different sheet and chill again for at least 20 minutes.

Preheat the oven to 175ºC/347°F/Gas mark 4.

Pop your cold baking trays directly into the hot oven and bake for 10–12 minutes, or until the pieces just start to turn dark brown at the edges. Smaller pieces will need a little less time. Allow to cool on the sheets.

Prepare the royal icing to stiff peak consistency according to the instruction on p.133 and colour it however takes your fancy. Put the icing into a piping bag. Colour your sugarpaste icing accordingly, if using.

Decorate your house pieces any which way you like! Silver or white sprinkles look great on the roof, or you can pipe individual bricks or shingles if you prefer. It is nice to add personal touches if you are giving the house as a gift – for example, by icing the house number onto the front door or the name of the street on the side of the house. Make sure all the pieces are dry before assembling.

To assemble your house, lay out all the pieces you will need and, using your super-stiff peak icing in a piping bag to act as your glue, pipe lines of icing on the edges of your pieces, and onto the bottom of the side and front panels too. See the photo to help you. Stick the front and side panels to the base, adding the back panel last and hold in place for a few seconds to set.

Allow the foundation walls of the house to set for about 10 minutes before adding the roof. The key here is more is more! More icing will help the house stay solid and in one piece, so don't be shy to stick it all together with plenty of icing – once it is put together you can cover up the joins with decoration if necessary.

Allow your house to set for 1 hour before packaging it up – either into a gift box or a large cellophane bag – and hey presto! A beautiful little house, ready to bite into.

GINGERBREAD SNOWFLAKES

MAKES ABOUT 14–18 COOKIES

<u>For the biscuits</u>
5 tbsp warm water
200g/7oz/1 cup light brown soft sugar
1 tsp allspice
2 tbsp each of ground ginger and cinnamon
2 tbsp each treacle (blackstrap molasses) and
    golden (light corn) syrup
250g/9oz/1 cup cold butter, cut into chunks
2 drops of orange essence or a few grates of
    orange zest (optional)
550g/1lb 4oz/4 cups plain (all-purpose) flour,
    plus extra for dusting

<u>For the icing</u>
1 batch soft peak Royal Icing (p.132), coloured
    with gold lustre, or paste food colours

I love gingerbread, which is lucky because I make it year round at the bakery! This recipe is German in origin, and I can honestly say it's the best I have ever tasted. You are welcome.

Put the water, sugar, spices, treacle and syrup into a saucepan (dip your spoon into hot water before you measure out and the syrups and treacle will slide off it easily). Mix gently and bring the mixture slowly to a simmer, stirring occasionally until a well-combined, glossy gloopy mixture forms and any sugar has melted in. Do not let it boil. Remove the pan from the heat and add the chopped butter and orange zest or orange oil, if using. Stir continuously until combined – it may look like it won't all mix in, but keep at it! Allow to cool slightly (you want it to be warm but not too hot to handle).

When it is cool enough to handle, pour the warm mixture into a large bowl and add most of the flour then bring together with a wooden spoon to a firm dough. If it feels too wet, add a little more flour but don't let it become too dry or crumbly.

Sandwich the dough between 2 sheets of clingfilm and roll the dough out. Chill in the fridge for at least 30 minutes to harden up.

Roll out the chilled dough on a lightly floured surface until it is just under 1cm/½in thick. Avoid dusting too much flour on the top. Using cutters, cut out as many pieces as possible from the dough. Place the cut pieces on a baking tray lined with parchment paper and chill in the refrigerator for another 20 minutes. Gather up the dough scraps and reroll, bearing in mind that cookies cut from scraps need extra time to chill to stop them spreading when they bake.

Preheat the oven to 175°C/347°F/Gas mark 4.

Bake the super-chilled cookies straight from the refrigerator for 8–10 minutes, or until the edges are just turning a darker shade of brown. Allow to cool on a wire rack before decorating.

To ice the biscuits, prepare your choice of coloured royal icing and stencils. Place your stencil over the top of the cookie and hold firm. Using a small palette knife or flat butter knife, gently scrape a small dollop of royal icing over the top of the stencil, making sure that the icing goes into every nook and cranny. Lift the stencil away gently and ensure it doesn't drag across the cookie as this will leave marks. Tidy up any messy edges with kitchen paper or the point of a sharp knife and allow to dry for about 1 hour before packaging or serving.

SPECULOOS

MAKES ABOUT 40 COOKIES
175g/6oz/¾ cup butter
225g/8oz/generous 1 cup soft brown sugar
4 tsp ground cinnamon
2 tsp ground ginger
¼ tsp ground nutmeg
¼ tsp ground cardamom or ground cloves
a generous pinch of sea salt and black pepper
420g/15oz/3 cups plain (all-purpose) flour,
   plus extra for dusting
70–90ml/2½–3fl oz/scant ¼–⅓ cup cold water

These little snappy, crunchy, spicy biscuits are one of my favourites. They are iconic in Europe and are often served with coffee in cafés, restaurants, trains and planes. In fact, they were only introduced to the US in the 90s when Delta airlines started serving them on their flights. They became so popular that the airline started selling them to US customers by mail order – that's a pretty popular cookie!

This recipe makes a lovely soft dough that will hold quite an intricate pattern if chilled thoroughly before baking.

Mix the butter, sugar, cinnamon, ginger, nutmeg cardamom, salt and pepper together in a large bowl until combined. Add half the flour and stir together, then pour in 70ml/ 2½fl oz/scant ¼ cup of the water and mix again. Add the rest of the flour and if needed, more water, a splash at a time, until it is a smooth, slightly sticky dough.

Form the dough into 2 slabs and sandwich each between 2 sheets of clingfilm. Using a rolling pin, roll it out until it is about 2cm/¾in thick, then chill in the refrigerator for at least

30 minutes to harden up. You can freeze one of the slabs if you want to save it for another time.

Roll out the dough on a very lightly floured surface to a nice even 5mm/¼in thickness then cut and emboss however you like. I used a chopstick for the person, a cooling rack for the heart and star, and a sugarpaste stamp for the snowflake. Remember to make a hole in the dough, so you can thread your cookie as a tree decoration, if you like. Arrange the cut cookies on a baking tray lined with parchment paper and chill again for another 30 minutes.

Preheat the oven to 160°C/325°F/Gas mark 3.

Pop your cold baking tray directly into the hot oven and bake for about 25–30 minutes, or until they turn a light golden around the edges. Allow to cool before eating.

These cookies absorb moisture in the air really fast, so make sure to store them in an airtight container and they will last for 2 weeks. If they do go a little soft, just pop them back in a hot oven for 5 minutes to crisp up.

AMARETTI BISCUITTINI

MAKES ABOUT 10–15 COOKIES AND 1 COCKTAIL

<u>For the Amaretti biscuittini</u>
2 egg whites
15ml/½ fl oz/½ tbsp Amaretto
170g/6oz/generous 1¾ cups ground almonds
170g/6oz/scant 1 cup soft brown sugar

<u>For the Biscuit Martini</u>
25ml/1fl oz/1 tbsp brandy
15ml/½ fl oz/½ tbsp Amaretto
2 tsp Frangelico
25ml/1fl oz/1 tbsp single (light) cream
25ml/1fl oz/1 tbsp milk
ice cubes

One of my first bakery employees was Nabil, a cocktail guru from the Savoy, and in the first winter of Bee's Bakery we would work a 12 hour Sunday shift in a freezing shared kitchen on an industrial estate... Needless to say, we spent a lot of time daydreaming and thinking up crazy ideas – including the 'Biscuittini', the one cocktail that would perfectly complement a biscuit!

Alex Kammerling from Kamm & Son's, arguably the best aperitif in the UK helped me realise this recipe for a delicious Biscuittini – try it, it's ace.

Preheat the oven to 175°C/347°F/Gas mark 4 and line a baking tray with parchment paper.

For the biscuits, put the egg whites into a large bowl and whisk vigorously until they form stiff peaks. If you have a stand or hand-held mixer, you are allowed to cheat with this recipe and use it! Add the Amaretto, then gently add the ground almonds and sugar, carefully folding them in until you have a smooth paste.

Using 2 teaspoons, spoon small, regularly sized rounds, about 3cm/1in apart onto the lined baking tray. If you feel like being really accurate, consider piping perfect rounds using a piping bag and a large open round nozzle. Bake in the oven for 12–15 minutes until the edges begin to brown. Cool before serving.

For the cocktail, pour all the ingredients into a cocktail shaker filled with ice and shake vigorously before straining into a martini glass. Garnish with an Amaretti biscuittini on a cocktail stick.

SALT AND PEPPER CHOCOLATE COOKIES

These are my homage to the classic, world-famous Oreo™ cookie, which I LOVE! These biscuits have an amazing history, being first made in 1912 by the National Biscuit Company in Manhattan, New York – the location is still called 'Oreo Way' to this day!

In a large bowl, crush the butter, flour and cocoa together between your fingertips until it resembles fine sandy breadcrumbs. Add the icing sugar and mix with a wooden spoon until just combined. Add the egg yolk, salt, pepper and vanilla and mix with the spoon until a smooth, fairly firm dough forms – it will be slightly sticky to the touch. If it's too crumbly, warm your hands and give it a gentle knead in the bowl to bring it all together.

Squeeze the dough into a flat sausage shape, and sandwich it between 2 sheets of clingfilm. Using a rolling pin, roll it out until it is about 2cm/¾in thick, then chill in the refrigerator for at least 30 minutes to harden up.

Roll the dough out on a heavily floured surface to about ½cm/¼in thick and, using a small circle cutter, cut out as many rounds as you can from that 1 sheet. You can emboss or stamp messages onto the tops of these cookies if you like, Using a palette knife, transfer the cut cookies onto a baking tray lined with parchment paper and chill again for 20 minutes.

MAKES AROUND 20 SMALL COOKIES
200g/7oz/scant 1 cup cold butter, cubed
265g/9¼oz/2 cups plain (all-purpose) flour, plus extra for dusting
35g/1¼oz/generous ⅓ cup cocoa powder
100g/3½oz/scant 1 cup icing (confectioners') sugar, sifted
1 egg yolk
1 tsp flaky sea salt
12–15 turns of your pepper mill
½ tsp vanilla bean extract
1 batch Vanilla Buttercream (see p. 129), coloured with paste colours (optional)

Preheat the oven to 170°C/338°F/Gas mark 3.

Pop your cold baking tray directly into the hot oven and bake for about 7–9 minutes, then allow the cookies to cool before decorating.

While they're baking, prepare your Vanilla Buttercream and colour some of it using paste colours, if you like. Pop the buttercream into a piping bag with a thin nozzle.

Once the cookies are cool, pipe a nice even layer of buttercream onto half of the cookies, remembering to flip them onto their backs first. I find piping in a spiral from the outside to the inside works well. Pop the tops onto these iced bottoms and chill in the refrigerator for 15 minutes. If you like, you can also roll them in sprinkles so they attach to the buttercream around the outsides before you chill them.

LIBERTY-PRINT COOKIES

MAKES 10–20 COOKIES
200–250g/7–9oz sugarpaste
  (ready-to-roll icing/fondant icing)
gel paste colours of your choice
icing (confectioners') sugar, for dusting
printed sheet of edible paper (see tip below)
piping gel
10–20 cookies of your favourite type of dough,
  baked and cooled

The department store Liberty of London has to be one of the most incredible buildings in London, built using the timber from two HMS ships in 1924. It has the most beautiful collection of iconic fabric prints and I have always coveted the Liberty print stationery sets – so gorgeous! These cookies are inspired by their iconic print designs, but of course you can print any design onto edible paper these days, so be creative! This one's for you Emma, Marco and Freccia the dog, who also features on p.123.

Colour the sugarpaste icing with a paste colour in any colour you like and roll it out on a surface dusted with icing sugar until it is 3–4mm/⅛–⅙in thick – make sure that the icing is larger than the printed sheet you are using. Paint the reverse of your printed sheet of edible paper evenly and thoroughly with piping gel, getting into every corner. Press your sheet down on top of the rolled icing and smooth it carefully, to make sure it sticks evenly and there are no bubbles.

Use the cookie cutters that you used for the cookies to press down firmly and sharply onto the icing sheet, a metal cutter is useful for this as it will be sharp.

Brush the top of your baked and cooled cookies with a little water and place the icing on top, gently smoothing it down. Allow to set on a wire rack before packaging up.

Tip
You can buy of sheets of printed paper from lots of online shops these days – I use the Cake Decorating Company (www.thecakedecoratingcompany.co.uk) for mine – they can print any high resolution image you like, or design something specific for you.

CRYSTALLISED FLOWER COOKIES

MAKES 8–12 COOKIES

For the cookies

8–12 pre-baked cookies of your choice, cooled and iced with a generous slather of stiff peak Royal Icing (see p.132) in a colour of your choice. I used a batch of Classic Vanilla Sugar Cookie dough (see p.18), with the grated zest of 1 lemon and 1 tsp chopped lavender flowers cookies added, covered with a pale pink royal icing.

For the flowers

several heads of edible flowers, such as violets, roses, pansies, nasturtiums, cornflowers, or dianthus

1 egg white

about 100g/3½oz/½ cup caster (superfine) sugar

I love working with edible flowers and each year, I create many wedding cakes and favour cookies using edible petals. It is important to source your petals and flowers from an organic grower so that you can be sure that they haven't been sprayed with poisonous (and nasty-tasting) pesticides – we get all of our petals from the super-cool Jan at Maddock's Organics, a flower farm in Devon, UK. In the photo, we have used a selection of fresh, dried and crystallised edible flower petals.

To dry out your flower petals, simply pull the petals away from the green stems, spread them out on a piece of parchment paper or on a tray, and leave somewhere airy, like your kitchen table overnight, or ideally for 24 hours. Do not dry them in the oven as the beautiful colours will be cooked out.

To crystallise your flower petals, pull a range of petals from the green stems, and separate them into individual petals, this is easier with larger petals. Pour your egg white into a shallow bowl, stir with a fork to break it up and gently dip each petal into it, making sure it coats the whole petal. What you're looking for here is a light covering of egg white, so try to shake off any extra egg white.

Put the sugar in a shallow bowl. Using a teaspoon, hold your dipped petal over the bowl of sugar and spoon the sugar over it, ensuring it covers the whole petal, then place the petal on a clean piece of parchment paper, and allow to dry overnight. You can then use these petals whole, or crush or chop them a little.

To attach the petals to the royal icing, brush a little of the leftover egg white, or water onto the areas of the cookie that you'd like to cover and gently press on a petal or two.

CHOCOLATE ORANGE BISCOTTI

MAKES ABOUT 15–25 PIECES OF BISCOTTI

115g/4oz/½ cup butter, softened but not melted
150g/5½oz/¾ cup sugar (caster/superfine keeps the mixture
   nice and pale, but soft brown is also fine)
grated zest of 1 orange or 2 clementines
2 large eggs
250g/9oz/½ cup plain (all-purpose) flour
1 tsp baking powder
2 tbsp orange juice
150g/5½oz/1 cup pecans almonds or hazelnuts, roughly
   chopped
150g/5½oz plain (semisweet) or milk chocolate, chopped into
   generous chunks
<u>To decorate (optional)</u>
50g/1¾oz plain (semisweet) chocolate, melted
gold sprinkles

Mix the butter, sugar and orange zest together in a large bowl with a wooden spoon until the mixture turns pale and a little fluffy. Add the eggs, one at a time, and keep stirring until smooth. Add the flour and baking powder and mix until combined.

Add the juice, nuts and chocolate and stir a final time – the dough will be really sticky, so dollop half onto a sheet of clingfilm and the other half onto a separate sheet. Form each half into a short fat log and chill in the refrigerator for about 30 minutes or 20 minutes in the freezer, until firm. Think about the shape of biscotti you are looking for here – if you like a more traditionally shaped biscotti, roll the log wide and shallow or if you like little round ones then roll into a long thin log shape.

Preheat the oven to 175°C/347°F/Gas mark 4 and line a baking sheet with parchment paper.

Transfer the chilled logs to the lined baking sheet, removing the clingfilm – this is most easily done by dusting your hands with flour. Bake in the oven for 25 minutes (15 minutes if you're going for a smaller round log) then allow to cool for about 20 minutes.

Lower the oven to 160°C/325°F/Gas mark 3.

Once cool enough to handle, slice the logs into 3–4cm/¼–1½in thick slices and turn the pieces onto their sides on the baking tray. A long bladed bread knife makes this very easy to do. Return to the oven and bake for a further 10–15 minutes until the slices are crunchy and are just starting to turn brown at the edges. Allow to cool.

If you like, drizzle the biscotti with melted chocolate, sprinkle with gold sprinkles and allow to set before serving.

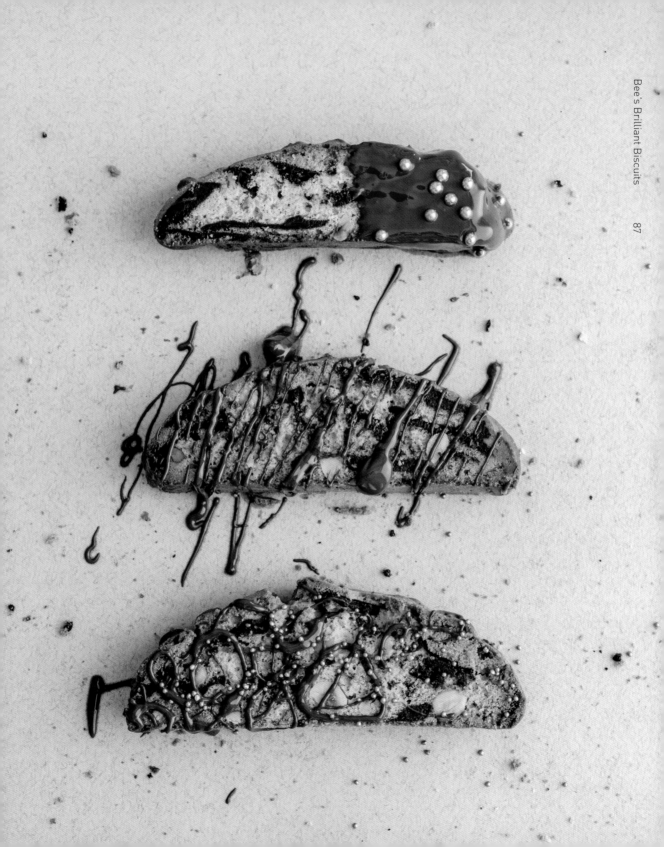

TUILES

MAKES ABOUT 12 TUILES
120g/4½oz/½ cup butter, softened
70g/2½oz/scant ⅔ cup icing (confectioners') sugar
4 egg whites, at room temperature
120g/4½oz/generous ¾ cup plain (all-purpose) flour, sifted
1 tbsp cocoa powder
paste food colouring (optional)

I first saw cookies like these in a Martha Stewart magazine article, and loved the idea of being able to write messages in your own handwriting onto cookies. I think that the colours look beautiful and I'm still amazed at how crisp the chocolate looks against the lighter coloured cookie. You could use these as thank you cards, or as wedding favours or even as awesome Christmas tree decorations.

For the template, take a piece of clean, thick card and cut out a shape from it with scissors, about 9–10cm/3½–4in across. I used a circle shape, but hearts, squares and rectangles also look cute.

Beat the butter and sugar together in a large bowl with a wooden spoon until well combined. Add the egg whites, one at a time, making sure that the mixture is smooth after each addition. Add the flour and mix gently until the mixture is just smooth and creamy.

Take about one-quarter of the mixture and, in a separate bowl, stir in the cocoa powder or food colour until it is a smooth evenly coloured mixture. Pop this into a piping bag with a Number 2 piping nozzle if you have one. If not, then use a freezerproof bag, with a very small and clean edged hole cut into one corner.

Preheat the oven to 160°C/325°F/Gas mark 3 and line a baking tray with parchment paper.

Place the template on the lined baking tray and, using a palette knife, spread a thin (2–3mm/¹⁄₁₆–⅛in) even layer of your white tuile mixture over the template, making sure you get the mixture into all the corners and edges. Gently lift the template away and check that you have a nice crisp shape left behind on the paper. Pipe patterns or messages onto the shapes using the coloured mixture in your piping bag.

If you can, try baking one tuile first, to check that the mixture is evenly spread enough and you like the way your writing comes out. Keep spreading and leave about 1cm/½in between shapes. Try to fit as many on the baking tray as possible.

Bake the tuiles in the oven for about 4–6 minutes, or until the edges are just starting to turn brown. When they come out of the oven the middles will be really soft still, but they do firm up. Remove from the tray carefully as soon as they come out of the oven. While they are warm, tidy up any rough edges with a sharp knife, or use scissors to trim the edges to make the best of your work! Allow to cool.

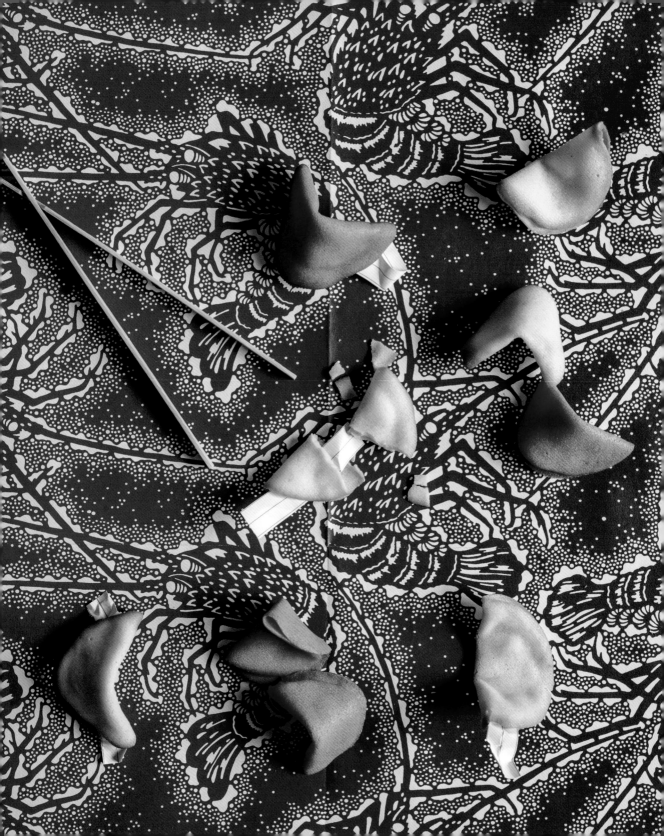

BRIGHTLY COLOURED FORTUNE COOKIES

The homemade fortune cookie is the winner of all personalised bakes, and once you get the hang of the folding bit, you will be hooked. This batter also takes colour really well, so go wild and bake some next-level fortune cookies for your mates!

MAKES ABOUT 15–20 FOLDED COOKIES
120g/4½oz/½ cup butter, melted, plus extra for greasing (optional)
4 egg whites
140g/5oz/scant 1¼ cups icing (confectioners') sugar
120g/4½oz/generous ¾ cup plain (all-purpose) flour
2 tsp almond extract
3–5 tbsp double (heavy) cream
gel or paste colours, as bright and as many as you like

Preheat the oven to 180°C/350°F/Gas mark 4. Line a baking sheet with a silicone baking mat or use parchment paper, greased well.

Before baking, make the 'fortunes' by writing messages or drawing little pictures onto tiny folded pieces of paper. Set aside.

Beat the egg whites and sugar together in a large bowl for 1 minute, then add the flour and mix until combined. Add the melted butter, almond extract and 3 tablespoons cream and mix again. You are looking for a consistency of thick pancake batter, so if needed, add more cream to make it more runny.

Drop 1 heaped teaspoon of batter onto the lined baking sheet and, using a spatula or butter knife, spread a very thin circle of batter into as perfect a circle as you can. You need an even coverage of batter, otherwise you will end up with some lighter and some darker patches when it bakes.

Bake this cookie first for about 4–6 minutes as a tester. This will enable you to finesse your technique before you use the rest of the batter. Bake for 4 minutes to start with and remove as soon as the little circle gets a touch of colour.

Remove the cookie from the oven and use a palette or butter knife to flip it onto its back. Place the 'fortune' into the middle of the cookie and gently fold it over into a half moon shape. Then, gently bend it into a 90° angle, holding it in place for a few seconds to set – work fast or the cookie will set hard and flat! Allow to cool.

If your cookies are too thick, they will be spongy and won't set hard when you fold them, so spread them thinly before baking. If they haven't baked enough, the cookies will be spongy and won't hold their shape, so bake for a little longer.

Once you have figured out what thickness is best, dollop and spread as much mixture as you can on your baking tray and then bake, fold and repeat until done!

CINNAMON ROLLS

When I asked my American and Canadian girlfriends which recipes from their side of the pond they would like to see in my book, these were top of the list! This one's for you Kate, Amy, Kat and Andrea.

In a large bowl, crush the butter and flour together between your fingertips until you have a mixture resembling fine breadcrumbs. Add both sugars and mix with a wooden spoon until just combined. Try not to overmix or you will end up with puffy misshapen biscuits. Add the eggs and vanilla and mix until your dough forms – it'll be slightly sticky to the touch.

Squeeze the dough into a flat sausage shape, and sandwich it between 2 sheets of clingfilm. Using a rolling pin, roll it out until it is about 2cm/¾in thick, then chill in the refrigerator for at least 30 minutes to harden up.

Meanwhile, make your filling and drizzle, covering with clingfilm before setting aside. Line a baking tray with parchment paper.

Roll out the dough on a floured surface to between 5mm–1cm/¼–½in thick – aim for a square shape of dough if you want a slightly fatter cookie after baking, or a longer rectangle if you like slightly smaller cookies.

Using the back of a teaspoon spread an even layer of the filling all over the rectangle of dough, right to the edges. Take one of the longer edges and start to form a nice tight and even roll. When you get to the end, transfer it to the lined baking tray, tucking the loose end underneath the weight of the roll to seal it. Chill the roll for 30 minutes.

MAKES 20 BISCUITS

For the cookies
165g/5¾oz/¾ cup cold butter, cut into cubes
360g/12¾oz/2½ cups plain (all-purpose) flour, plus extra for dusting
150g/5½oz/¾ cup caster (superfine) sugar
25g/1oz/¼ cup icing (confectioners') sugar
2 eggs
½ tsp vanilla bean extract

For the filling
20g/¾oz/1½ tbsp butter, soft but not melted
100g/3½oz/½ cup soft brown sugar
1 tsp ground cinnamon

For drizzling (optional)
30g/1oz/2 tbsp cream cheese
30g/1oz/2 tbsp butter, soft but not melted
140g/5oz/1¼ cups icing (confectioners') sugar
½ tsp vanilla bean extract
1–2 tbsp milk
juice of ½ lemon

Preheat the oven to 165°C/329°F/Gas mark 3 and line a baking sheet with parchment paper.

Cut the roll into individual cookie pieces and arrange them on the lined baking sheet, making sure that they are 2cm/¾in apart. If you have any misshapen rolls, squeeze back into shape before baking.

Bake in the hot oven for about 8–10 minutes, or until the edges are just starting to colour. Allow to cool for a few minutes before drizzling, which you can do by brushing the glaze all over the top of each cookie with a pastry brush, or you can pipe nice straight lines with a piping bag, if you like.

VIENNESE WHIRLS AND SWIRLS

These whirls are the perfect return on investment. They are a simple, one-bowl wonder recipe. The shapes are quite easy to pipe, and with a bit of care and attention they look and taste so impressive. You can swirl them and whirl them your way, dip, drizzle or fill them however you like, so get your thinking cap on and have some fun! They taste delicious as part of an afternoon tea or an after dinner treat.

Put the butter into a pan and heat until it is very soft, just on the verge of melting, then transfer to a large bowl. Add all the remaining biscuit ingredients and mix well with a wooden spoon until smooth.

Spoon the mixture into the piping bag fitted with a large star-shaped nozzle. If you like to add a stripe of colour, then do this now by smearing some paste colour down one side of the piping bag before filling it with the biscuit mixture. Have a practice piping rosettes onto a baking tray lined with parchment paper. Aim for shapes that are about 6cm/2½in across. If it takes you a couple of goes to get the right shape, just scrape the mixture off the tray and shove it back into the bag! Chill the piped shapes in the refrigerator for 20 minutes.

Preheat the oven to 170°C/338°F/Gas mark 3.

Pop your cold baking tray directly into the hot oven and bake for 12–14 minutes until the edges are just starting to colour and the tops feel like they are firming up. Allow to cool.

If you want to dip or drizzle the cookies in melted chocolate, do this when they are cool and allow to set before you fill them with buttercream and jam. Spoon a little smudge of buttercream onto one of the inverted rosettes. Dollop a little jam on top, then gently sandwich with the cookie lid. Put the biscuits on a baking tray and chill in the refrigerator for 5 minutes to set.

MAKES 12–15 WHIRLS

For the biscuits
250g/9oz/generous 1 cup salted butter
50g/1¾oz/scant ½ cup icing (confectioners') sugar
250g/9oz/1¾ cups plain (all-purpose) flour
40g/1½oz/generous ¼ cup cornflour (cornstarch)
½ tsp vanilla bean paste
paste food colouring (optional)

For the filling
1 batch Vanilla Buttercream (p.129)
75g/2¾oz/⅓ cup seedless jam e.g. raspberry

For dipping (optional)
100g/3½oz plain (semisweet) or milk chocolate, melted

Viennese Whirls pictured here with Basque Tea Biscuits (p.96).

BASQUE TEA BISCUITS

MAKES 12–15 BISCUITS

250g/9oz/generous 1 cup butter, melted
100g/3½oz/scant 1 cup icing (confectioners') sugar, sifted,
  plus extra for dusting (optional)
grated zest of 1 orange and 1 lemon
  or lime, plus extra for decorating (optional)
1 egg, plus 1 egg yolk
320g/11½oz/2¼ cups plain (all-purpose) flour, sifted
20g/¾oz/scant ¼ cup cornflour (cornstarch)
100g/3½oz plain (semisweet) chocolate, melted,
  for dipping or drizzling (optional)
a few strips of citrus zest
  or icing (confectioner's) sugar (optional)

My big sister and her family have lived in the French Basque country for years and so I have spent a little bit too much time loitering around some of the patisseries there – with specialties like Gateaux Basque, a lush, cherry jam-filled tart, and these lovely little snack cookies that are often dipped in chocolate. They are really easy to make and you can be quite creative with piping different shapes, or even letters.

Preheat the oven to 180°C/350°F/Gas mark 4. Line 1–2 baking trays with parchment paper.

Put the butter, sugar and citrus zest into a large bowl and mix vigorously with a wooden spoon until well combined. Pour in the egg and yolk and mix again energetically until everything is very well combined. Add the flour and cornflour to the mixture and stir gently and carefully until it is just combined, scraping down the sides as you need to.

Prepare a piping bag with a large closed star nozzle and spoon in the mixture. Be creative and pipe lots of different shapes, from swirls to lines, to your initials, to squiggles and star shapes or zigzags onto the lined baked trays. Try to keep all the shapes on one tray roughly the same size so that they bake evenly.

Bake in the oven for 15–18 minutes until the edges start to colour and they are nice and crispy. Allow to cool, then decorate them by dipping them into melted chocolate. You could also add a few strips of citrus zest, or simply sprinkle a little icing sugar on top.

SECRET RUBIK'S CUBE COOKIES

These are a bit of a mind-boggler... but only until you make them and then it feels like you are in a delicious biscuitty 'clever club'. Give them a try, then try to keep them a secret!

MAKES ABOUT 30 COOKIES
400g/14oz/1¾ cups cold butter, cut into pieces
700g/1lb 9oz/5 cups type '00' flour (pasta flour)
300g/10½oz/scant 2⅔ cups icing (confectioners') sugar
2 eggs
grated zest of 1 large orange, or 4–6 drops orange essence
4 different paste colours (I used yellow, pink, green and blue)

Pop all the ingredients, except the colouring, into a large bowl and use your fingertips to crush the butter and mix, pressing the dough together with your hands until it forms a firm ball – this is hard work, so get your playlist on!

Divide your giant ball of dough into 4 balls and weigh them to get them as close to 355g/12oz each as possible – it is very important to get this bit right!

Colour each ball to your preferred tone with paste colours, kneading until you have a nice even colour.

Using a pencil and a ruler, draw four 18cm/7in squares on a piece of parchment paper, then carefully roll each dough ball to perfectly fit each square. Tuck in the edges, cut off and re-position any bits of dough that go outside the lines to ensure that you have as perfect a square of dough as is humanly possible at 1cm/½in deep – no pressure!

When you have your 4 perfect squares, cut each into 3 pieces measuring 18 x 6cm/ 7 x 2½in with a sharp knife. Do use a ruler for this bit to be precise.

Put 2 large pieces of clingfilm on the work surface, then lift a piece of dough carefully onto each with a palette knife. Brush the tops of these with water and place another coloured piece of dough on top of each. Repeat until you have two 6 x 6cm/2½ x 2½in blocks of dough. Try to make sure that you are not mirroring the pattern on each stack, and that you don't have two colours next to each other. Make sure that all of your edges and corners line up and you have 4 nice flat sides. Wrap these 2 stacks up in clingfilm and chill in the refrigerator for 30 minutes.

If you like, you can now cut your stacks into 1cm/½in thick slices across the short ends, and then you will have lovely stripy cookies, but why not keep going to get the full Rubik's cube effect?!

Using a ruler, mark out even 1cm/½in scores down the length of your stacks and carefully and evenly, cut straight and even sized slices along the length of each.

When both stacks are cut into 6 slices each, you can start to re-assemble the 6 x 6cm/ 2½ x 2½in blocks by layering them up with a light brush of water between each. Try to avoid having the same colours next to each other as you stack – if you turn some of your slices 180 degrees before layering that will help. Again make sure that all your edges and corners line up and you have 4 nice flat sides. Wrap in clingfilm and chill again for 30 minutes. Alternatively, you can freeze one of your blocks for using later.

Preheat the oven to 170°C/338°F/Gas mark 3 and line a baking tray with parchment paper.

Slice your stack along the short edge at regular 1cm/½in intervals to reveal an awesome Rubik's cube-style square cookie! Put these onto the lined baking tray and bake for about 12–15 minutes, or until there is a hint of colour on the edges. Allow to cool before serving and knock everyone's socks off!

WOVEN SHORTCRUST PASTRY

MAKES UP TO 20 WOVEN COOKIES
250g/9oz/1¾ cups plain (all-purpose) flour
50g/1¾oz/scant ½ cup icing (confectioners') sugar, sifted
125g/4½oz/½ cup cold butter, cut into pieces
2 tbsp crushed dried rose petals
1–2 tbsp rose water
1 egg
a splash of milk
1 tsp vanilla bean extract
2 tsp crushed culinary lavender flowers or
  1 tbsp chopped basil leaves and grated zest of 1 lemon
  (optional)

I love to combine crafting skills and baking, and this is the perfect way to do both – I think these cookies look fantastic! When you add floral flavours to a sweet shortcrust pastry and bake it just as you would a biscuit, it has on a lovely short, crunchy bite, perfect with a big mug of steaming Earl Grey tea.

Sift the flour and icing sugar together onto your work surface to make a mound. Make a hole in the middle and put the butter into it. Using your fingertips, crush the butter into the dough until it is a crumbly sandy pile of breadcrumbs. Sprinkle the crushed rose petals onto the pile, and drizzle the rose water over the top.

Add the egg, splash of milk and the vanilla and gently work together until it is a smooth ball of dough. Don't overwork the dough.

Sandwich the dough between 2 sheets of clingfilm. Using a rolling pin, roll it out until it is about 3cm/1¼in thick, then chill in the refrigerator for at least 30 minutes.

Line a baking tray with parchment paper.

Divide the dough into 2 portions – one about two-thirds of the whole dough and the other one, a third. Roll out both portions to about 3mm/⅛in thick, keeping the dough moving as you roll to make sure it is even. Roll the smaller piece of dough into a long thin rectangular shape and the larger one into a large circle.

Keep the dough in position on the work surface, then using a long-bladed sharp knife, cut both portions of dough into long thin strips, about 1cm/½in wide – a chopping motion is easier than a scoring motion here.

Using the larger piece of dough first, imagine there's a horizontal line about halfway across. Working from the top, fold alternate strips of dough downwards towards you with the bend at the 'halfway' line. At this point you will have every other strip of dough folded downwards. Now take one of the strips from the smaller piece of dough and lay it horizontally across the middle of the bigger piece, just above the fold. Move the strands you folded back up over the new strips you have just placed down,

tucking them in tightly with no gaps. You will see that it starts to look woven. Now fold down the remaining strips as you did before – laying another horizontal piece of dough on top. Repeat until you have a fully woven piece of dough, and then complete the bottom half in the same way. Once done, gently press down on the woven dough using your hands or rolling pin to help to seal the weave in place.

Using your favourite cookie cutter, cut out as many shapes as you can from the woven dough, cutting right to the edge to save work!

Transfer these pieces carefully to the lined baking tray, tucking any stray strands back into place. Roll up your dough scraps and repeat the process until it is all used up. Rest the cookies in the refrigerator for at least 30 minutes in the fridge.

Preheat the oven to 170°C/338°F/Gas mark 3.

Pop your cold baking tray directly into the hot oven and bake for 10–12 minutes until the edges are just starting to turn brown. Allow to cool on a wire rack before eating.

SHORTBREAD FRUIT PIES

MAKES 8–12 TARTS
2 x batches Go-to Shortbread
 recipe (see p.19)
butter, for greasing
plain (all-purpose) flour,
 for dusting
1 large free-range egg,
 beaten

For the fruit pie filling
50g/1¾oz/3½ tbsp butter
100g/3½oz/½ cup golden caster (superfine)
 sugar, plus extra for sprinkling
2 Bramley or other cooking apples, cored,
 peeled and cut into chunks
4 Cox apples, cored, peeled and cut into the
 same sized chunks as above
150g/5½oz/1 cup blackberries, blueberries or
 other dark fruits
½ tsp ground cinnamon

This little fruit tart topper was inspired by a beautiful lace effect cake I once saw, where hundreds of individual 2D sugar flowers were layered onto a wedding cake. This technique is really lovely. You could use star shapes at Christmas, or any other shapes, so be creative!

Prepare the shortbread dough according to the instructions on p.19 and chill in the refrigerator for at least 30 minutes before using.

Put the butter and sugar into a large pan and melt the butter gently over a low heat. Once melted, tip in the apples and cook at a gentle simmer for about 15 minutes, or until the apples are soft but not disintegrating. Add the berries or other fruit and cinnamon and cook for 5 more minutes, gently mixing with a wooden spoon to ensure that the fruit is broken down into small, regularly sized pieces. Drain the fruit, reserving the juices.

You are now ready to make your shortbread bases, so grease a 12-hole cupcake or muffin tin or individual tart tins. Measure how big a shape you will need fill them and choose the right cutter or size of mug.

Roll out the chilled dough on a floured surface to about ¾cm/¼in thick. Using the best-sized cutter, cut out about 12 rounds and use to line the tins. Using the remaining dough, cut out about 30–40 small and medium sized shapes, such as small flowers, and set aside.

Your fruit mix will have cooled by now, so put into a bowl and consider whether you want to add in any of the reserved juice. You are looking for a thick consistency, with some small visible chunks of fruit, so if you need to add in a little of the juice then do so, but don't let it become too runny or the cookie bases won't cook.

Preheat the oven to 170°C/338°F/Gas mark 3.

Put a heaped spoonful of fruit mixture into each of the cases, almost to the top of each. Make sure the filling is flat then put your cut-out shortbread shapes on top, going for a layered effect as some will sink into the fruit. Brush the tops with a little beaten egg.

Bake for about 20 minutes, or until the fruit is bubbling away nicely and the shortbread shapes are brown on top. Allow to cool before removing from the tins.

SUGAR AND GLUTEN-FREE OATY COOKIES

Yes I'm a baker, so stereotype dictates that I don't have a huge problem with eating a lot of sugar, butter and gluten – true story! However, if I can make something delicious and full of energy, which just happens to NOT contain a huge amount of these things, then that's a bonus for me. My friends Debs and Stu swear by these cookies as fuel on long bike rides, as they provide great slow-release energy.

In a large bowl, thoroughly combine the apple sauce, mashed banana, cinnamon, oats and almonds. Allow to rest for at least 10 minutes so the oats begin to soak up the moisture and the mixture thickens.

Preheat the oven to 170°C/338°F/Gas mark 3 and line a baking tray with parchment paper.

Add the chopped nuts and dried fruit to the bowl and mix well. Add the milk, 1 tablespoon at a time, until it is a slightly gloopy mixture that's very sticky. You may not need all of the milk. Spoon equally sized dollops onto the lined baking tray – go for nice round shaped dollops and squish them down a little bit in the middle. Sprinkle some seeds on top for a crunchy texture, if you like and bake in the oven for 20–25 minutes until the edges are crispy and the tops are slightly golden brown. Serve straightaway, or store in an airtight container for up to 3 days.

MAKES ABOUT 10–12 COOKIES

220g/8oz/1 cup apple sauce (available in most large supermarkets)

1 large ripe banana (even better if it is overripe), peeled and mashed until smooth

1 tsp ground cinnamon

1 tsp vanilla extract

90g/3¼oz/1 cup rolled or porridge oats (the more budget the better, as they'll be nice and crushed up)

45g/1½oz/½ cup ground almonds

50g/1¾oz/⅓ cup chopped nuts, such as almonds, walnuts, hazelnuts and pecans

50g/1¾oz/⅓ cup dried fruits of your choice, such as raisins, cranberries, dates and prunes

2–3 tbsp milk (using soya milk makes this recipe vegan)

1 tsp seeds, such as poppy seeds, chia seeds, sesame, pumpkin and pine nuts (optional)

Tip

If you prefer, you can bake these cookies as a 'bar' by pouring the mixture into a lined square 20 x 20cm/8 x 8in brownie tin or a 450g/1lb loaf tin and increase the bake time by 5 minutes.

Apple sauce is available in jars from most supermarkets or you can make your own by gently cooking about 2 peeled apples cut into cubes in a pan until they make a nice gooey appley mash with no big lumps.

GLUTEN- AND DAIRY-FREE AVOCADO CHOCOLATE COOKIE

MAKES 6 LARGE COOKIES

1 ripe avocado (when it's peeled and stoned you'll need around 100g/3½oz)

1 egg

150g/5½oz/¾ cup light brown soft sugar

40g/1½oz/scant ½ cup cocoa powder

40g/1½oz plain (semisweet) or milk chocolate, melted

a pinch of salt

50g/1¾oz/scant ½ cup gluten-free flour (any combination of the following
   flours will work – standard GF flour, rice flour, gram flour)

1 tsp vanilla bean paste

½ tsp xanthan gum (optional – without this, your cookie will be crumblier)

1 tsp bicarbonate of soda (baking soda)

80g/3oz plain (semisweet) chocolate, roughly chopped

I'm quite into substituting dairy, gluten and white sugar in baking for less unhealthy alternatives, but ONLY if the change isn't noticeable and you still have a super-tasty bake…, which often isn't the case. With these cookies though, it's different, they are genuinely one of my favourite chocolate cookie recipes. Before baking, the mixture tastes like a mouthful of front lawn, (seriously, try it!), but afterwards, they are gooey, soft and really chocolatey, just what you are looking for.

Preheat the oven to 180°C/350°F/Gas mark 4 and line a baking tray with parchment paper.

Scoop the avocado flesh into a large bowl and thoroughly mash until a smooth green goo is formed – no lumps please! Add the rest of the ingredients to the bowl and beat with a wooden spoon until a shiny consistent wet mixture is formed. It will look like a very sticky and dark coloured cake batter rather than a firm cookie dough. If you taste a little of the mixture at this point, you will be amazed at how 'green' it tastes, but after baking, the vegetable taste is gone. Add most of the chocolate chunks, reserving some of the larger pieces to press into the top of each cookie before baking.

Using 2 metal spoons, dollop even sized round shaped cookies onto the lined baking tray – larger is always better with these ones, and they don't spread much when baking. If you prefer a thicker fudgier cookie, pile the mixture high and be prepared to bake for the full time. If you like a thinner chewier cookie then spread it out more and bake for less time. Press a couple of chocolate chunks into the top before baking and bake in the oven for 12–15 minutes. Allow to cool. The cookies will still be slightly soft to the touch when done, but firm up and go nice and gooey after cooling.

PB&J THUMBPRINTS

MAKES ABOUT 14–16 SMALL COOKIES
<u>For the cookies</u>
180g/6oz/generous ¾ cup crunchy
   peanut butter
100g/3½oz/7 tbsp butter, softened but
   not melted
120g/4½oz/scant ⅔ cup soft brown sugar
1 egg
1 tsp vanilla bean extract
150g/5½oz/1 cup plain (all-purpose) flour
½ tsp baking powder

<u>For the jam puddles</u>
About ½ a jar of smooth
   jam, such as raspberry or
   smooth strawberry

These gorgeous little cookies are real crowd pleasers – I haven't met anyone who doesn't like them yet. They are also pretty easy to make, and if you have a little person to help with poking the holes in the middle, that's even better.

Preheat the oven to 175°C/347°F/Gas mark 4 and line a baking sheet with parchment paper.

In a large bowl, mix the peanut butter and butter together until smooth, then add the sugar and mix until pale and fluffy. Add the egg and vanilla extract and mix until combined, then add the flour and baking powder and bring the dough together.

Using an ice-cream scoop or 2 dessertspoons, pop equally sized dollops of mixture onto the lined baking tray, leaving 2cm/¾in between dollops as they will spread a little during baking. Bake in the oven for 8 minutes, then remove the cookies from the oven and carefully use the end of a wooden spoon to press a dimple into the middle of each one.

Return the cookies to the oven and bake for another 5–8 minutes until they just start taking on some colour. If the middle has risen when you take them out of the oven, just re-make the dimple with the end of your spoon. Allow to cool then drop ½ teaspoon jam into the dimple in the middle and serve!

Store your cookies in plastic containers and they will last for almost a week.

CRAZY IN THE COCONUT COOKIES

MAKES 12–18 COOKIES

90g/3¼oz/scant ¼ cup coconut oil, melted but not hot
255g/9oz/generous 1¼ cups soft brown sugar
1 tsp vanilla bean extract
3 tbsp milk (either or almond or rice milk)
¼ tsp baking powder
a pinch of salt
150g/5½oz/1 cup plain (all-purpose) flour (coconut, wheat
   or any mixture of gluten-free flour is fine – consider part
   ground almonds flour, part gram flour, part rice flour),
   plus extra for dusting

There is a lot in the media about the potential health benefits of coconut, so I wanted to give baking with coconut oil and flour a go. While I wouldn't advocate swapping butter for coconut oil all the time (!) I do think it's important to give dairy alternatives and vegan cookies a try every now and again. The coconut flavour in these little cookies is intense if you use both the flour and oil, so if you are not a huge fan of a strong coconut vibe, I have suggested some alternative flours you can use to bring the flavour down a bit.

In a large bowl, mix the coconut oil and sugar together until smooth, about 2 minutes. Add the vanilla then the almond or rice milk, 1 tablespoon at a time, and mix until it is incorporated. Add the baking powder, salt and most of the flour and mix thoroughly, Check the consistency of the dough – you are looking for a soft dough that isn't gloopy or too dry. This all depends on the temperature of the coconut oil, so add a little more flour if it feels too wet, or a little more milk if it feels too dry.

Roll out the dough straightaway onto a lightly floured work surface, to about 1.5cm/⅝in thick. Cut out as many shapes as you can and arrange on a baking tray lined with parchment paper. Use up your scraps (add a little almond or rice milk if it's too dry) by re-rolling and cutting. Chill the cut shapes in the refrigerator for 20 minutes

Preheat the oven to 175°C/347°F/Gas mark 4.

Pop your cold baking tray directly into the hot oven and bake for 8–10 minutes depending on their size – larger cookies might need a wee bit longer. Allow to cool on a wire rack.

CANDIED BACON AND CHOC CHIP COOKIES WITH A MAPLE GLAZE

Preheat the oven to 200°C/400°F/Gas mark 6 and line a baking tray with parchment paper.

To candy your bacon, lay it out on the lined baking tray and sprinkle both sides with soft brown sugar. Bake in the oven for 10–15 minutes until it is cooked and a little bit charred on the edges. Allow to cool, then using scissors, cut the bacon into different sized pieces, both big and small. Scrape the parchment paper and save any crunchy bits for adding to the cookies.

To make your cookies, beat the sugar, butter and vanilla together in a bowl until light and fluffy then add the egg and mix until combined. Add the flour and baking powder and stir until the mixture is smooth. Add the chocolate chips and bacon pieces, reserving some for decoration.

Preheat the oven to 180°C/350°F/Gas mark 4 and line another baking tray with parchment paper.

Put regularly sized dollops of the cookie mixture onto the lined baking tray, leaving 5cm/2in between each as they will spread a little when baking. Bake for about 20–25 minutes until the edges just start to colour and take on a little crunch.

Meanwhile, prepare the maple glaze by mixing the maple syrup and icing sugar together in a bowl until smooth. Syrups are often different consistencies, so if you need to add a little more syrup, or a little more sugar to get the right drizzle consistency (think double cream), that is fine!

Allow the cookies to cool before drizzling with the maple icing and sprinkling the reserved candied bacon bits on top.

MAKES 10–12

For the candied bacon
200g/7oz smoked, streaky bacon, thick cut if you are really going for it!
4 tbsp soft brown sugar

For the cookie dough
250g/9oz/1¼ cups soft brown sugar
140g/5oz/scant ⅔ cup butter, softened but not melted
1 tsp vanilla extract
1 egg
240g/8½oz./1¾ cups plain (all-purpose) flour
1 tsp baking powder
140g/5oz good-quality plain (semisweet) chocolate, roughly chopped into chunks

For the maple glaze and decoration
4 tbsp maple syrup
2 tbsp icing (confectioners') sugar

RED CHEESE AND POPPY SEED BISCUITS

These cookies are inspired by Dan Lepard, whose fantastic Red Leicester biscuit recipe I tore out of a newspaper years ago and still have now. This biscuit is perfect for picnics or as a canapé, and also looks gorgeous packaged up in a little cellophane bag tied with a ribbon – a fantastic stocking filler if you like!

Put the butter, flour and seasonings into a large bowl and use your fingertips to break down the butter chunks and combine them with the flour and seasonings until it starts looking like a loose cookie dough. Add the cheese and begin to bring the dough together by kneading it gently inside the bowl – as it gets warmer it will come together to form a stiff, slightly speckled dough.

Tip the dough onto a lightly floured surface and start to form it into a long thin cylinder, about 6–8cm/2–3in across. Try to keep it nice and uniformly round across the length.

Spread the seeds of choice onto a piece of clingfilm and gently roll the dough over the surface so that the seeds attach to the outside edges. Wrap the dough in clingfilm and chill in the fridge (or freezer) for 20 minutes until firm.

Preheat the oven to 175°C/347°F/Gas mark 4 and line a baking tray with parchment paper.

MAKES 10–12, DEPENDING ON THE SIZE OF CUTTER USED

125g/4½oz/½ cup cold salted butter, cut into chunks

170g/6oz/1 cup plain wholemeal (whole-wheat) flour, plus extra for dusting

a pinch of flaky sea salt

1 tsp freshly ground black pepper (it needs to be coarse)

¼ tsp cayenne pepper or chilli powder

¼ tsp chilli (red pepper) flakes (optional – only if you can handle the heat!)

160g/5¾oz/1⅓ cups red cheese, such as Double Gloucester or Red Leicester, finely grated

½ packet (50g/1¾oz) poppy seeds, for rolling

Use a sharp knife to cut regularly sized circles of dough about 1.5cm/⅝in thick and put these onto the lined baking tray. Tidy up any bald patches of exposed cookie dough by pressing seeds into the dough. Bake in the oven for about 20 minutes, or until the tops of the cookies are nicely rounded and are starting to turn golden brown. Allow to cool before eating, if you can wait that long!

Tip

If you don't like poppy seeds, try black sesame seeds, caraway seeds or onion seeds, or a mixture of all.

BBQ BACON BISCOTTI

This might just be my favourite biscuit in the whole book! It was inspired by my neighbour Michael, a brilliant American barbecue chef from Kansas City. He makes beautiful barbecue sauces and rubs for his company Prairie Fire. I think you will agree that these are pretty cool. Mike, this one's for you...

Gently knead almost half of the barbecue sauce into the cookie dough, then divide the dough in half and divide one of the halves in half again.

Colour the largest piece of dough a strong mid-pinky red colour, and one of each of the smaller pieces a darker brown red colour and the other a lighter yellowy colour.

Roll out the pieces of dough into the shapes you like on a floured surface, and assemble and layer up the different pieces however you like – brush a little bit of the barbecue sauce in between each layer to seal it. Try to go for a pretty random stacking of colours, perhaps with the darkest one on top, and the lightest one at the bottom – try to get a marbling effect in the middle with a thick line of fat. If you go wrong, then just peel or scrape off the layers of dough and start again!

For the top, darkest layer of dough, finish it by giving the top of the log a really thick brushing of barbecue sauce, and then a good sprinkle of meat rub and sugar mix to seal it. Wrap the dough in clingfilm and chill in the refrigerator for at least 1 hour.

Preheat the oven to 170°C/338°F/Gas mark 3 and line a baking tray with parchment paper. Create ridges with some folded parchment paper or foil – these will create the bend and twist in the dough that you would normally see in a crisped-up rasher of bacon – and put on the parchment paper.

Use a very sharp, long bladed knife to cut regular, thin slices from the dough and arrange them over the ridges on the lined baking tray. Bake in the oven for about 8–12 minutes, depending on the thickness of the dough. Allow to cool on the ridges to get a realistic bacon-y effect!

MAKES ABOUT 14–16 SLABS OF BISCUIT BACON

about 100ml/3½fl oz/scant ½ cup good-quality barbecue sauce, preferably hot and spicy (I use Prairie Fire Sauce)

1 batch Classic Vanilla Sugar Cookie dough (see p.18) or Speculoos dough (see p.77)

food colouring pastes in pink, red, brown and yellow

plain (all-purpose) flour, for dusting

1 sachet of barbecue meat rub, mixed with a little caster (superfine) sugar

SEEDED CRACKERS

MAKES 10–20 CRACKERS, DEPENDING ON SIZE
360g/12¾oz/generous 2 cups plain wholemeal (whole-wheat)
  or plain (all-purpose) flour, plus extra for dusting
2 tsp sugar
2 tsp flaky sea salt
4 tbsp good-quality olive oil
230ml/8 fl oz/1 cup cold water
salt and freshly ground black pepper
3 tbsp seeds of your choice, such as sesame, poppy, pumpkin,
  black onion, fennel, or a combination of all

Crackers for cheese are so fun to make and so easy to personalise to your taste that, once you have tried them, you won't bother with boxed crackers ever again. Bold claims, but justified! The most important thing is getting the right consistency – too sticky and they will be a nightmare to roll, but too dry and they will get all misshapen in the oven.

Preheat the oven to 225°C/437°F/Gas mark 7 and line a baking sheet with parchment paper.

Mix all the ingredients, except the seeds, together in a large bowl with a wooden spoon until a soft, sticky dough forms.

Roll out the dough onto a sheet of parchment paper until it is about 3–4mm/⅛–⅙in thick. Brush the top of the dough lightly with water and generously sprinkle the seeds evenly over the top. Season with plenty of salt and pepper.

Using a sharp knife, cut the cracker sheets into squares, diamonds or long thin strips, trying not to cut through the paper. Slide the parchment carefully onto your baking sheet. Prick the tops with a fork to create holes for steam to escape without puffing up the dough and making it all misshapen and bake in the oven for about 12–15 minutes (smaller ones will take less time).

When you remove them from the oven they should crack crisply, not bend or still feel wet. If they do, just pop them back into the oven for another 5 minutes. Allow to cool.

These crackers will store well for about 2 weeks in an airtight container and are delicious with a dip like hummus, or a slab of cheese on top.

Tip
It might be easier to roll out the dough in smaller portions rather than rolling it all out in one go. If the dough is sticky then dust your rolling pin as well. Try to make sure that the dough is the same thickness. To do this keep changing the direction in which you roll your dough.

HOMEMADE TEETHING RUSKS

MAKES ABOUT 15–20 RUSKS
DEPENDING ON THE SIZE YOU NEED

½ a ripe banana, the more bashed up
the better!
45g/1½oz/3 tbsp butter or margarine
45g/1½oz/scant ¼ cup light brown soft sugar
1 egg
100g/3½oz/¾ cup wholemeal (whole-wheat)
flour
1 tsp baking powder
½ tsp ground cinnamon

I have taken it upon myself to be the first to introduce several of my girlfriends' babies to their first biscuit – it's my duty! Quite often it's been a factory-made, branded, packaged up baby rusk, albeit an organic one of course... but I did think, these things can't be THAT hard to make surely? So here's a pretty quick recipe, without too much bad stuff and just enough flavour.

Preheat the oven to 160°C/325°F/Gas mark 3 and line a baking tray with parchment paper.

Mash the banana in a bowl until it is smooth and light and bubbly in texture.

In another bowl, cream the butter and sugar together until it is as light and fluffy as you can get it – it needs to be really pale in colour. Mix in the egg and banana until combined. Add the flour, baking powder and cinnamon and mix until it is just combined. Keep as much air in the mixture as possible – it will be a pale and pretty wet dough.

Using wet hands or 2 spoons, form chunks of the dough into long and thin rusk shaped pieces, and arrange these on the lined baking tray. Bake in the oven for about 20–25 minutes until they are totally dried throughout. If they are still a little soft in the middle, switch off the oven and leave them in there for another 10 minutes to dry out. Store in an airtight container.

DIY DOG BISCUITS

MAKES 20–25 DOG BISCUITS,
  DEPENDING ON SIZE
300g/10½oz/generous 1¾ cups wholemeal
  (whole-wheat) flour, plus extra for dusting
1 egg
2 tsp beef or chicken bouillon granules
5 rashers (slices) of cooked streaky bacon,
  or a small handful of any of the below,
  according to your dog's tastes:
  cooked chicken or other meat, cheese,
  oats, eggs, etc.
200–240ml/7–8½fl oz/scant 1–1 cup warm
  water

This is Freccia, she is my absolute favourite hound on the planet, and I have the utter pleasure of taking care of her from time to time. I think that her owners Emma and Marco know she has restorative powers for me, so I wanted to come up with a healthy home-made treat for her to say thank you, and luckily, she loved these biscuits, as you might be able to tell!

Preheat the oven to 180°C/350°F/Gas mark 4 and line a large baking tray with parchment paper.

Put all the ingredients, except the water, into a large bowl and mix until everything is combined. Pour in half of the water at first, then mix, then add another splash and mix again – repeat until a stiff, non-sticky dough is formed.

Roll out the dough on a lightly floured surface and cut out your preferred shape of biscuit – putting them onto the lined baking tray. Bake for 7–10 minutes until the biscuits start to brown at the edges.

Allow to cool before serving. Serve only as an occasional treat.

Note: Different breeds have different food tolerances, so do check the ingredients against what you know your dog's tummy can tolerate. If your dog is new to you/borrowed/on a strict diet, please check with the owner/a vet before serving.

BUCKWHEAT AND MINT DOG BISCUITS

MAKES 10–20 BISCUITS DEPENDING ON SIZE
180g/6oz/1½ cups buckwheat flour,
 plus extra for dusting
4 tbsp finely chopped fresh parsley
2 tbsp finely chopped fresh mint
1 tbsp honey
2 tbsp olive oil
1 egg, beaten
1–3 tsp warm water

I am 100 per cent a dog person and have quite a few friends and family who have rescue dogs – the best kind of puppy! I can't wait until the day comes when I can get a little rescue pooch to keep me company in the office, but for now, I have to settle on baking these fun treats for my four legged friends of friends.

Preheat the oven to 200°C/400°F/Gas mark 6 and line a baking sheet with parchment paper.

Put all your ingredients, except the water, into a large bowl and stir until mixed together. Add 1 teaspoon warm water and knead gently until a dough is formed. If you need to add more water then do so sparingly and don't let your dough become too wet.

Roll out the dough on a lightly dusted surface to about 1.5cm/⅝in thick. Cut the dough into shapes with a small cutter or use a sharp knife to cut into small squares.

Put the biscuits on the lined baking sheet and bake for about 15 minutes until the biscuits are dried out. Wait until cool before serving. Go easy on your portions, 1–2 biscuits at a time is plenty. Store the biscuits in an airtight container.

Note: Different breeds have different food tolerances, so do check the ingredients against what you know your dog's tummy can tolerate. If your dog is new to you/borrowed/on a strict diet, please check with the owner/a vet before serving.

ICING & FROSTING

VANILLA BUTTERCREAM ICING

MAKES ENOUGH FOR 1 BATCH OF COOKIES

160g/5½oz/1⅓ cups icing
  (confectioners') sugar,
  sifted
150g/5½oz/⅔ cup salted
  butter, softened but not
  melted (you can substitute
  vegetable margarine or
  vegan spread if you like)
2 tsp vanilla bean paste

Optional extras:
  add 2 tsp lemon or orange or lime zest
  pour in 3–4 drops orange or almond essence,
    rose water or peppermint essence
  replace 25–35g/1–1¼oz/scant ¼–⅓ cup icing
    (confectioners') sugar with cocoa powder
    for a chocolatey twist
  add a sprinkling of crushed rose petals or
    finely ground culinary lavender for a floral note

A good, reliable buttercream is to baking what the colour black is to fashion – it goes with everything. Here's your staple buttercream recipe, with some optional additions if you fancy a bit of a change.

If you have a stand or hand-held mixer, use it for this recipe – either that or face guaranteed baking biceps, as it will take a bit of energy!

Slowly and gently combine the icing sugar, butter, vanilla and any extra flavours together. If you are doing this by hand, mix the icing sugar into the butter in thirds, otherwise it will fly everywhere and create an icing sugar storm in your kitchen. If you are using a mixer, place a clean tea towel over the bowl to stop the sugar storm.

When everything is combined and there are no lumps, this is the time to really give it a thrashing – whip the mixture around at full speed for at least 5 minutes by hand, or 3 minutes using the mixer. Scrape down the sides regularly, and keep going until you notice that the mixture has become much paler in colour, and is light and fluffy in texture.

You can chill any leftover buttercream, just remember to remove it from the refrigerator 1 hour before you need it, and give it an energetic mix before using to smooth any bubbles out.

LEMON, ORANGE OR MAPLE DRIZZLE ICING

MAKES ENOUGH ICING FOR 1 BATCH OF COOKIES
20g/¾oz/2 tbsp caster (superfine) sugar
90g/3¼oz/generous ¾ cup icing (confectioners') sugar, sifted
grated zest and juice of 1 lemon or ½ orange
1–2 tbsp maple syrup, depending on taste (optional)

Pop both sugars and the grated zest into a large bowl and add about half the juice. Mix until combined, adding in extra juice until you have a thick consistency, a little like double cream. Stir in the maple syrup, if using.

CHOCOLATE GANACHE

MAKES ENOUGH GANACHE FOR 1 BATCH OF COOKIES
200g/7oz/scant 1 cup double (heavy) cream
200g/7oz plain (semisweet) or milk chocolate

Heat the double cream in a saucepan over a medium heat until it just gently comes to a simmer.

Meanwhile, chop your chocolate into regularly sized small pieces and put them into a large heatproof bowl.

When the cream is ready, pour it on top of the chocolate pieces and scrape out the pan to make sure you have every drop of cream, then whisk gently until you have a lovely thick shiny chocolate goo.

You can use this ganache in several ways:
• As soon as it has melted, pour or drizzle it on top of cookies.
• Once it's cooled a little and thickened, spread it on top of cookies with a palette knife for a pretty but rough-style icing finish.
• Once it has cooled completely, use a piping bag to create piped swirls or fill cookie sandwiches.

Store the ganache for a week in the refrigerator or up to 2 months in the freezer.

SWISS MERINGUE BUTTERCREAM

**MAKES MORE THAN ENOUGH
FOR 25 COOKIES**
2 egg whites
120g/4½oz/scant ⅔ cup caster (superfine)
 sugar
250g/9oz/generous 1 cup butter, at room
 temperature and chopped into pieces
1 tsp vanilla extract

Warning: this recipe really does need a hand-held or stand mixer – it's really, really hard work without one! Use this buttercream in the same way you would use ordinary buttercream, bearing in mind that its super-buttery and much more susceptible to heat than normal.

Put the egg whites and caster sugar into a heatproof bowl set over a pan of gently simmering water and whisk until the sugar is totally melted into the egg white, which will be warm and frothy at this point. Transfer the mixture to a freestanding mixer with a whisk attachment, or put into a bowl and use an electric whisk instead. Whisk at high speed for about 3–4 minutes until the mixture is super-white in colour and forms stiff peaks, and the bowl is cold.

Turn the mixer to medium speed and add the butter, a couple of small pieces at a time, waiting for each bit to be mixed in before adding more. Don't worry if your mixture looks like it has split at any point, just keep adding the butter and it will come back together. Add the vanilla extract and whisk briefly until combined.

Store the icing for a week in the refrigerator or up to 2 months in the freezer.

ROYAL ICING

MAKES ENOUGH FOR DECORATING 1 BATCH OF COOKIES
2 egg whites, or powdered egg white (check the packet
    instructions if making a different quantity of icing)
a squeeze of lemon juice, about ¼ lemon
500g/1lb 2oz/4⅓ cups icing (confectioners') sugar, sifted
piping gel, as needed (if you are planning on intricate piping
    work, this stuff is a good investment as it makes the icing
    flow more easily)

As well as being the perfect icing to use for decoration and piping work, royal icing is the edible glue of the biscuit world – there are three different consistencies that we use most regularly at Bee's Bakery and I have outlined how to make each of them below.

This is probably the only recipe that I would use a freestanding mixer for if making it at home, as it is really hard work to get a smooth stiff peak icing. So, if you have one, go ahead and make it useful. Otherwise, flex your muscles and get ready for some real work Arnie!

Put the egg whites, lemon juice and piping gel, if using, into a large bowl and mix just to combine. Tip in half of the icing sugar and mix gently. If you are using a stand mixer then cover the open bowl with a clean tea towel to avoid the icing sugar flying all over the place!

Keep adding the icing sugar until you have a super-thick, creamy and smooth mix – you do need to give it some welly here and keep scraping down the sides of the bowl to make sure it all combines – it will look thick and glossy but not wet when it is done.

As royal icing will set hard if exposed to the air, I usually keep my icing in an airtight container, and cover the icing with a new piece of jiffy cloth or several layers of damp kitchen paper.

STIFF PEAK

Per the recipe opposite, this icing consistency
is used to glue tiers of cookies together, such
as in my Mini Wedding Cake Cookie (see p.63).

SOFT PEAK

Per the recipe on page 132, with water added drop by drop and 1 teaspoon piping gel, stirred in until a slightly softer icing is formed that still holds its shape. This is used for outlining cookies, piping detail or messages on top, such as on the Rangoli Piped Cookies (see pp.61–62). When ribboned in the bowl, this icing ribbon will sink into the main pool of icing after about 10 seconds.

FLOOD ICING

Soft peak icing with even more water added
results in a consistency a bit like double cream.
When ribboned in the bowl, this icing ribbon
will sink into the main pool of icing after
5–10 seconds. I use this when decorating
my Party Rings (see p.46).

QUESTIONS & ANSWERS

Q: How do you fix a crumbly dough that won't hold together?

A: There are two things that could be wrong here – either your butter is too cold, or there's too much flour in the recipe or on the work surface. Try taking out a handful of crumbs and squidging them between the palms of your hands for a couple of minutes. If you feel the dough coming together as your hands heat up the ingredients then work the rest of the dough in the bowl with your hands and it should come together. If this doesn't work, then try adding an extra egg yolk – the master of all baking glue! Again, work the dough with your hands to squeeze, mush and cajole it into staying in one piece.

Q: What's Bee's favourite cookie recipe?

A: My favourite has always been my Jammy Dodger (see pp.31–33), it was the first really cool baking idea I came up with (in my opinion!) and it still has a wow factor that I'm really proud of! A close second is my 'Trash Can Cookie' (see p.41) – I love that it is totally customisable to any whim and the mixture of salty and sweet flavours really floats my baking boat.

Q: How do I make a biscuit with Earl Grey tea?

A: You're in luck here – the answer is very simple. Add 1 teaspoon of the contents of a good-quality teabag or ground or chopped loose tea to your standard vanilla dough… easy peasy. Tea is safe to consume when from a reputable supplier, and there is a recipe for this on p.66.

Q: What's the best way to store biscuits?

A: Always in an airtight container like a biscuit tin or plastic container. You can also store them unbaked or baked in the freezer for up to a month – this is especially good for broken biscuits if you want to recycle them and use them in another recipe later – see p.58 for a cool idea.

Q: How long can you store a biscuit iced with royal icing?

A: Royal iced biscuits lasts for ages, at least 2 weeks, if kept in an airtight container. The trick is to make sure that the icing and biscuit are completely dry all the way through as any leftover water will help bugs and bacteria grow, causing mould. You can speed this process up by popping your biscuits into an oven preheated to 50°C/122°F/lowest possible Gas mark for about 30 minutes. Gingerbread lasts even longer, at least a month, and I actually think that the flavours improve with age!

Q: What's the best, super-quick recipe to make with kids?

A: The most annoying thing for kids is having to wait for the cookie dough to chill, so go for recipes that don't need this, like my Honey and Oatmeal recipe (p.26). Alternatively, my Lemon Sugar Cookie Roll recipe (p.20) is meant to be frozen, then sliced and baked straight from the freezer – you can even pre-cut it before freezing, then the little ones only have to take a few slices out, pop them on a tray and bake from frozen, with some adult assistance of course. There are more tips for baking with kids on p.15.

Q: How do you get that gooey middle in a cookie?

A: This is all about choosing the right recipe, and then ever so slightly under-baking the middle. With a shortbread recipe, you are never going to get a really gooey middle – the best recipe for this is my Ultimate Gooey Chocolate Cookie (p.51), the 'Trash Can Cookie' (p.41) or the Honey and Oatmeal Cookie (p.26). I always bake to the minimum time on the recipe, then take the cookies out and after a couple of minutes, check that they are the right level of gooey-iness for you – if not, return them to the oven for a few more minutes – easy peasy! It's useful to remember that you can always bake for a few more minutes if you need to, but once they are overdone and crunchy there's no going back.

Q: How can I make sure that my biscuits bake evenly?
A: Always bake at the minimum temperature on the recipe – remember you can always put cookies back into the oven for a few minutes, but once they are overdone it's too late. Then, become friendly with your oven! Next time you bake or cook something, have a look at what comes out the oven carefully – you might find that certain areas of your oven are hotter than others, for example, where the fan blows the hot air out. Bear this in mind when baking cookies – if there's a particularly hot area then put a thicker or bigger cookie there, or even consider leaving a gap on your tray to avoid the problem completely!

Q: How do I stop my cookies from going flat in the oven?
A: This could be happening for one of a few reasons – most recipes need you to chill your cookies for at least 20 minutes before baking to help them keep their shape, and it's always best to put your cookies onto a chilled baking sheet, not a warm one straight out of the oven. If this has been done and they are still spreading, then either the butter and sugar combo has been overworked, or, if they are crispy and bubbly at the edges, then there is too much butter or sugar in the recipe. Try adding a little bit more flour to the mixture, and try to only mix your dough until just combined, not knead it into submission!

Q: What difference does it make what oven shelf I use?
A: It makes TONS of difference! Hot air rises, so the top of your oven will always be hotter than

the bottom. Get used to switching trays around when baking and you should quickly be able to find the perfect position for an even bake.

Q: Some of my cookies are thick, and cool slowly, and some are thin so get burnt – help!
A: It sounds like your dough rolling technique is a wee bit lopsided here! This is really common – when I'm rolling out, often my edges are thinner and my middle is thicker, so I know to always give one final roll to the middle part. When you are rolling out, make sure there is enough flour underneath to enable you to lift and turn your sheet of dough. Do this every few rolls, and turn it about a quarter of the way around. Scooch down and get on a level with your sheet of dough to check that you have an even thickness throughout, and correct this if not.

Q: My biscuits always burn on the bottom – why?
A: Are you using good-quality parchment paper? This is a good prevention method for a burnt cookie bottom, and even better still, think about investing in a silicone mat, which will almost certainly stop burning the bottom of your biscuit.

Q: One of my biscuits on the tray always burns – why?
A: You probably have a hotspot in your oven, or you are rolling certain biscuits thinner than the rest. Try to roll more evenly (see Q above on this) and consider leaving a gap on your baking sheet to avoid this problem in the future.

Q: My biscuits are far too hard – why?
A: This might be because your oven is running hot and you are overbaking them without

realizing it, so try turning the oven down and putting your baking tray a bit lower down in the oven. Another factor could be that your eggs are too big – try using medium ones instead.

Q: My biscuits are unbaked in the middle, and burnt on the edges – what's happening?
A: The temperature of your oven is probably too high – bring it down by 10 degrees and check on it every few minutes once its been in the oven for the minimum bake time to see if this helps.

Q: I've tried to substitute gluten-free flour in recipes before, but they always end up tasting sandy and dry – what can I do?
A: Gluten-free flour is really tricky, and the best way of counteracting this dusty taste that I have found is to incorporate ground almonds where possible, as they add moisture, texture and flavour. Try to use at least two types of gluten-free flour instead of the pre-mixed packs you can buy – for example, rice flour, gram (chickpea) flour and coconut flour. A bit of flavouring also helps, such as a drop of two of orange, almond or lemon essence. I have a super gluten-free Lemon Shortbread recipe on p.22.

Q: How do I make a vegan cookie?
A: The simplest answer is... by following my recipe for Avocado and Chocolate Cookies on p.106! In general, you can get away with using a vegetable margarine in all of my softer cookie recipes, and there are plenty of these without eggs. Try to chill these substituted recipes well or even better freeze them before baking to help them hold their shape.

Q: What's the best ratio of flour/cornflour/ rice flour for a really good shortbread recipe?
A: Try my shortbread recipe on p.19 – it's got great crunch and is quite 'short'. If you're looking for a gluten-free version, then try my Lemon Shortbread recipe on p.22.

Q: How can I tell when my biscuits are baked enough?
A: First of all, always bake for the shortest time on the recipe then take them out and have a check. For lighter coloured cookies, it's easy to check – just take your tray out and carefully use a palette knife or butter knife to lift the edge up slightly. If there is some colour on the bottom of your biscuit, then it's probably done. With darker coloured cookies, or gooey ones, go easy on the baking time and take them out when the edges are just starting to feel crispy – remember you can always put them back into to the oven for a few minutes if you need to, even if they've cooled down.

Q: I used a cookie cutter but my biscuits came out misshapen – why?
A: This is probably because you are rerolling your dough too often, or not chilling the cookies enough before baking. Try to always cut out as many cookies from each sheet of rolled dough as you can and avoid rolling more than three times. If you are definitely doing both of these things and still having problems, then do a bit of 'prettifying' after they are baked! Use a cheese grater to shave off any lumps, bumps or burnt edge, no one will ever know!

Q: When I roll out my dough, it always sticks to the work surface, no matter how much flour I put down – why?
A: It sounds like you're not moving the dough around when you roll, so try this: When rolling out, after every few rolls, put your rolling pin in the middle of your dough and pull one edge over it, rolling towards you as you go. This will help you pick up your dough so you can re-dust the underneath. Place the dough back on the work surface in a different position, to make sure you're correcting for any pressure unbalance while you're rolling.

Q: What can you do with broken biscuit pieces?
A: Lots of things – never throw them away; it's a terribly waste! I suggest that you put them into a freezer bag and store them in the freezer until you have a few handfuls. Check out my recipes for using up broken biscuits on p.58.

Q: How can I stop the biscuits in my tin going soft?
A: Get a better tin! No seriously, it might not be airtight, which is causing a problem. A quick fix for this is to re-bake your cookies just before serving, a quick blast of 10 minutes at a temp of about 150°C/300°F/Gas mark 2 should sort them out.

INDEX

STOCKISTS

Baking kit: Nisbets (www.nisbets.co.uk) and Lakeland (www.lakeland.co.uk) both sell a good range of basic baking kit. Harts of Stur sell alphabet cutters. A Piece of Cake Thame sell a good range of baking and decorating kit.

Aprons: Without a doubt the coolest apron makers around are Hedley & Bennett. www.hedleyandbennett.com

Printed images: www.thecakedecoratingcompany.co.uk

Rubber stamps, bespoke and themed: The English Stamp Co. (www.englishstamp.com)

Ingredients: Always use free range eggs, no excuses. And fairtrade sugar. Source honey from local beekeepers where possible.

Edible flower petals: Jan at Maddocks Farm Organics has the most beautiful edible flowers (www.maddocksfarmorganics.co.uk)

Nut butters: Try to buy fairtrade or organic nut butters, we use Pip and Nut, made by the lovely Pip herself!

Tea: Any organic tea is safe for human consumption, but I like to use Joe's Tea, made by my friend Joe, the best brew in the land!

ACKNOWLEDGEMENTS

I have been dreaming about writing a book for a while, so a big thank you to everyone who has encouraged and supported me, put up with my procrastinating jibber jabber, high-fived and celebrated with me, and eaten my test bakes (some of which were a bit weird) during the writing process!

Thank you to Milly Withington at Capel & Assoc. and Lola her dog who appears on p.125. Big cheers to Emily Preece-Morrison my editor boss lady who at no point said 'that's ridiculous' even when my ideas were exactly that. Nice one to my creative dudes Charlie Phillips with the best props (and hair!) you have ever seen; photographers Liz and Max Haarala Hamilton (Carhartt4ever!), and a super big thanks to my right-hand woman Laura holding the reins back at the ranch. To Helen ducky egg, for endless support in and outside of my baking life; to Louise my word-guru; and to my army of recipe testers, especially Debs and mum. Thank you to Dominique, Millie and Caitlin for being the best interns ever.

Props to my first-ever baking team, Millie and Nabil, who I'm sure will never forget the blisters and bicep strains we got cutting 1,000s of Jammies in that first bleak winter of Sunday bake offs. Big up to James the sausage roll man, Reshmi the macaron queen, Gary and Phil and all my neighbours at the kitchen unit – you have saved me with loaned ingredients way more than I deserve, and you all work really hard and give small food business a great name!

Love and thanks goes to my main man Dan, who deals with the perils of being Mr Bee's Bakery whilst being my biggest cheerleader too. He never complains about me, our house or car constantly smelling of gingerbread, or biscuit crumbs found in unmentionable places, and he is at constant risk of the most hazardous of all side effects, the dreaded 'bakers belly'!

PUBLISHER'S ACKNOWLEDGEMENTS
Thanks to Max and Lix Haarala Hamilton for photography, Charlie Phillips for prop styling, Kathy Steer, Laura Russell and Maru Studio.

First published in the United Kingdom in 2016 by Pavilion
1 Gower Street
London
WC1E 6HD

Text © Bee Berrie, 2016
Design and layout © Pavilion Books Company Ltd, 2016
Photography © Pavilion Books Company Ltd, 2016

ISBN: 978-1-91049-646-6

A CIP catalogue record for this book is available from the British Library.

10 9 8 7 6 5 4 3 2 1

Reproduction by Tag Publishing UK
Printed and bound by 1010 Printing International Ltd, China

This book can be ordered direct from the publisher at www.pavilionbooks.com

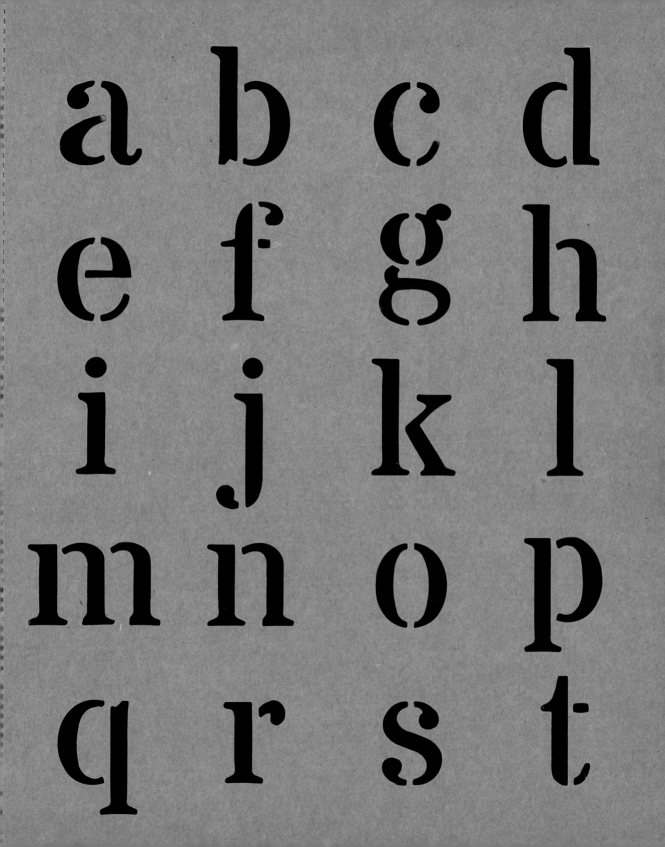

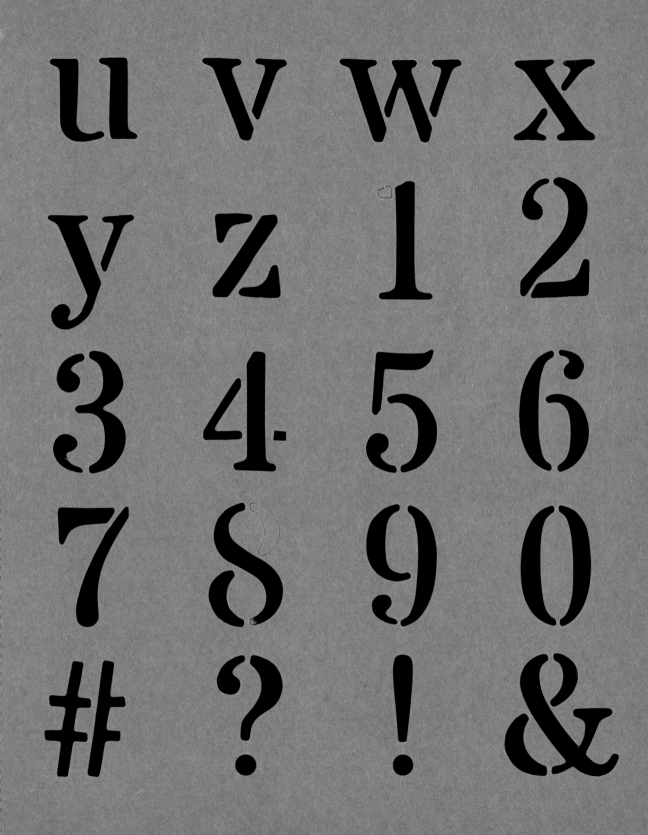

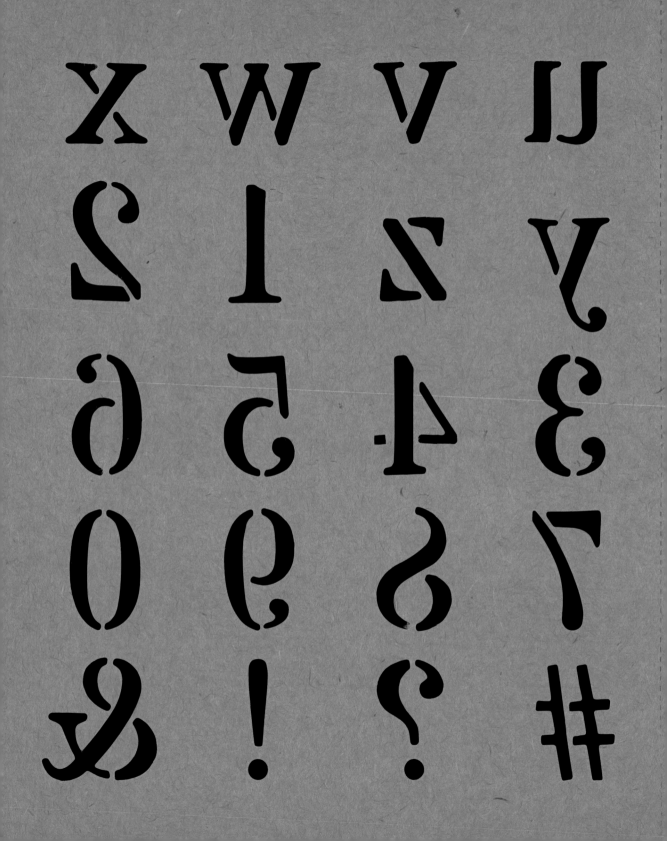

About Bee Berry

The brains behind the best jammy dodgers in London, Bee Berrie is an ex-microbiologist who swapped bacteria for baking full time in 2012. In just a few years Bee's Bakery has grown from a home kitchen business to being named one of the top five biscuit bakeries in London by the *Evening Standard*. Bee has created a giant replica Kinder Egg for ITV, appeared on Channel 4 with Heston Blumenthal and been filmed for advertising campaigns for Ralph Lauren and Olay. She's baked bespoke cookies and cakes for clients including the BBC, Topshop, Jamie Oliver and Harrods and created an enormous baked perfume bottle for Marc Jacobs.

Known for her bold, design-led baking, Bee's biscuits have appeared in many publications including *Stylist, Red* and *Brides* magazines, *Evening Standard*, *The Observer*, *Stella magazine* and the *Guardian*. She is a regular contributor to www.JamieOliver.com and has appeared on YouTube as a guest presenter, and on FoodTube presenting collaborative recipes.

'Cookies and biscuits are everything that cupcakes are not!' she says. 'Extremely versatile and quick to make, they last for ages, and there are tons of parent recipes that are super easy to adapt and customise to make something truly original.'

www.beesbakery.co.uk